SING

YOUR

FAITH

The Lindsey Press
The General Assembly of Unitarian
and Free Christian Churches

Published by The Lindsey Press on behalf of
The General Assembly of Unitarian and Free Christian Churches
Essex Hall, 1-6, Essex Street, London WC2R 3HY

www.unitarian.org.uk

First published in Great Britain in 2009 — 10 yrs ago

ISBN: 978-0-85319-077-6

Joint Editors
Andrew M. Hill   David Dawson

Printed in Great Britain by
Pioneer Press Ltd, Unit 2, Airedale Business Centre
Enterprise Way, Keighley Road, Skipton BD23 2TZ

CONTENTS

PREFACE

INTRODUCTION

Most British Unitarian congregations use *Hymns for Living* (1985) [the green book] or *Hymns of Faith and freedom* (1991) [the red book] or *Y Perlau Moliant Newydd* (1997) [the black book]. All three books have served the denomination well and will continue to do so. However, much new material has become available in recent years which needs to be made available for contemporary Unitarian worship. *Sing Your Faith* is a digest of this new material drawn from many sources, including hymns from *Let Us Sing* (1994) and from recent American Unitarian Universalist books: *Singing the Living Tradition* (1993), *Singing the Journey* (2005) and *May this Light Shine* (2006). Other hymns come from recent collections by other denominations, from internet surfing, and from hymn writers and composers themselves.There is a significant contribution from living British Unitarians. The Hymn Book Working Group collected and sang through close to 500 hymns ending up with 231.

WORDS

Hymns are often suitable for more than one occasion; for this reason the traditional hymnbook arrangement according to subjects and seasons has been replaced by an alphabetical sequence supported by a detailed subject index. This subject index is, however, no substitute for a thorough knowledge of the collection, and regular users will want to add to and/or create their own personal subject references.

The open and non-creedal nature of Unitarian and Free Christian Churches makes a hymnbook significant for visitors and inquirers seeking insights into Unitarian and Free Christian thought and practice. A small collection of 'words for worship' has been included to further this purpose.

There is a wide variety of hymn formats and language in this collection. Hymns may be addressed to the worshipping community:

'Let us . .' or to a divine other 'You are . .' or to the best in oneself 'May I ..'. Hardly a single text examined used exclusively male imagery for God. God as 'Mother' (141), 'Midwife' (110) and 'Goddess' (86) are now in common usage, a fact that has allowed us to be less concerned about occasional masculine imagery where it occurs e.g. 'Warm father God' (14). Some hymns revel in using a variety of images. The fertile imaginations of some contemporary Christian writers, such as Brian Wren and Shirley Erena Murray, often makes their work more accessible for Unitarians and Free Christians.

Climate and ecology, and earth as 'a garden' are prominent features, as are webs and weaving and songs for blessing partnerships and relationships. Some hymns refer to several faith traditions and a few actually draw imagery from them. A noticeable feature is the number of hymns with 'incarnational' themes, recognising bodies as sacred and 'made in all sizes', valuing touch and reminding us that love does not batter, neglect or abuse.

Traditionally hymns have been written in certain standard metres with interchangeable tunes. As an aid to escaping this rigidity we have followed the modern convention of not using capital letters for every line but only at the start of sentences. In addition there are now many more hymns which have broken away from rigid regularity by using unusual and irregular metres.

MUSIC

A hymnbook is first and foremost about words – words that speak clearly and imaginatively to a contemporary congregation. Music's role is to enhance those words and provide an accessible vehicle for group expression.

In selecting music for this hymnbook we have aimed for a wide range of musical styles using keys more in keeping with current group vocal range. Whilst all the words are 20th/21st century, it would be unrealistic to apply such a criterion to the music. There are 'traditional' hymn tunes, particularly where authors have written specifically for such tunes; and, where musically appropriate, we have tried to use tunes that for various reasons were little used in previous British Unitarian hymnbooks.

Many hymns and their tunes are written to a regular metre; this metre is indicated alongside the name of the tune. There is an increasing trend now to write outside the common metrical patterns. In the past such tunes were described as 'irregular'. In this book, where no meter is given, it should be assumed either that the metre is irregular or that the words and the musical setting are inseparable.

No speeds are indicated. In general, and where musically appropriate, we have used the crotchet (quarter note) pulse and a 2/2 time signature to imply and encourage a more energetic pace. We do not indicate the type of accompanying instrument. Some tunes are clearly more pianistic in style, but should be adaptable for more traditional church accompaniment or other instrumental resources. We have tried to keep to a modest level of difficulty in order to enhance accessibility and we thank copyright holders for sometimes allowing simpler arrangements of their work. By tradition the church musician will always have the freedom to add, subtract and adapt the written score in performance.

Traditionally, in British Unitarian hymnbooks, the tunes and the words have been printed separately, primarily to retain visually the overall cohesion and poetry of the words. In this book a more pragmatic approach has been adopted with some of the less familiar tunes having the first verse of the words written 'inside' the music – it may then be repeated with the other verses. Occasionally all the words are written 'inside' the music. This is usually done for page layout reasons and to avoid turn-overs.

COPYRIGHT

Since this is a twentieth and twenty-first century hymnbook copyright issues have featured prominently. We have succeeded in contacting the copyright holders of almost every hymn text and tune used. For those few instances where no copyright holder has been identified or where no response has been forthcoming, copyright has still been acknowledged and any conditions will be fulfilled should they be made known to the publishers. We are grateful to all those who gave their permission for us to use their work, either as a gift or for small fees.

FINALLY

We trust that you will, in an adventurous spirit, explore, enjoy, and use the words and music in this hymnbook.

THANKS

We wish to thank our colleagues on the Hymn Book Working Group: Peter Sampson, Alan Myerscough, Kate Taylor and Wynne Simister; and, in the early stages of preparation, Andrew Brown and the late Arthur Long. Our thanks also go to Myrna Michell for proof-reading.

Joint Editors:

Andrew M. Hill
David Dawson

Hymns 1 to 220
are arranged in alphabetical order
according to the first line of the text.

Short responses and rounds are
from 221 to 231

TRUE RELIGION 10.8.10.8.

Jim Reilly, b.1943

1.A core of sil - ence breathes be - yond all words, or else the words have lit - tle worth; to 'heart' or 'soul' or 'spir - it' it comes forth (the words we name them mat - ter not).

The 'small' notes have been added to the original score for those wanting a fuller arrangement.

1 A core of silence

A core of silence breathes beyond all words,
or else the words have little worth;
to 'heart' or 'soul' or 'spirit' it comes forth
(the words we name them matter not).

And half the music lies within the pause
between the arches of the heart;
the print upon the page means less than ink
unless the white and black both speak.

The 'true religion' gathers up its text:
'In the beginning was the Word.'
But I seek quietness behind that start
and name it nothing, much less 'God.'

Jim Reilly b. 1943

WAS GOTT THUT 88.88.8.

Severus Gastorius, c.1675
Harmony: David Dawson

1.A prom-ise through the ag - es rings, that al - ways, al- ways,
some - thing sings. Not just in May, in finch - filled bower, but
in De- cem - ber's cold -est hour, a note of hope sus - tains us all.

2 A promise through the ages rings

A promise through the ages rings,
that always, always, something sings.
Not just in May, in finch-filled bower,
but in December's coldest hour,
a note of hope sustains us all.

A life is made of many things:
bright stars, bleak years, and broken rings.
Can it be true that through all things,
there always, always something sings?
The universal song of life.

Entombed within our deep despair,
our pain seems more than we can bear;
but days shall pass and nature knows
that deep beneath the winter snow
a rose lies curled and hums its song.

For something always, always sings.
This is the message Easter brings:
from deep despair and perished things
a green shoot always, always springs,
and something always, always sings.

Alicia S. Carpenter b. 1930

THE SALLEY GARDENS 76.76.D.

Traditional Melody
Arr. David Dawson

1.A - bove the moon earth ri - ses a sun - lit, mos - sy stone, a gar - den that God priz - es where life has rich - ly grown, an em - er - ald sel - ec - ted for us to guard with care, an isle in space pro - tec - ted by one thin reef of air.

Note: *Salley* is an anglicisation of the Irish *saileach*, meaning *willow*.

Music © 2009 Arrangement used by permission.

3 Above the moon earth rises

1st verse is with the music

The mossy stone is grieving,
its tears are bitter rain,
the garden is unleaving
and all its harvests wane,
the emerald is clouded,
its lustre dims and fades,
the isle of life is shrouded
in thick and stagnant haze.

O listen to the sighing
of water, sky and land,
and hear the Spirit crying,
the future is at hand:
the moss and garden thinning
portend a death or birth,
the end or new beginning,
for all that lives on earth.

A death if hearts now harden,
a birth if we repent
and tend and keep the garden
as God has always meant:
to sow without abusing
the soil where life is grown,
to reap without our bruising
the sunlit mossy stone.

Thomas Troeger b. 1945

SHIPSTON 87.87.

Collected by Lucy Broadwood, 1858-1929
Harm. Ralph Vaughan Williams, 1872-1958

4 All that is abundant living

All that is abundant living,
all that is the world's delight,
all that is our costly giving,
all the world's transforming light,

all the darkness and the shadow,
all the depth of soil and earth,
all the sleepers in the hedgerow,
all that waits to come to birth,

all that's doubtful and uncertain,
all that may not be quite true,
all that hides behind the curtain,
all that's unsure what to do.

These with care we hold and handle,
these we gently put in place,
these we keep from vice and scandal,
these we bless in every case.

Andrew McKean Hill b. 1942

5 All the colours

DE COLORES

Spanish Folk Tune

1. All____ the col - ours,__ yes, the col - ours we see in the
2. All____ the col - ours,__ yes, the col - ours of peo - ple pa-
3. All____ the col - ours,__ yes, the black and the white and the

spring-time with all of its flow - ers. All__ the col- ours, when the
rad - ing on by with their ban - ners. All__ the col- ours, yes, the
red and the brown and the yel- low. All__ the col- ours, all the

sun-light shines out through a rift in the cloud and it show- ers.
col - ours of pen -nants and stream-ers and plumes and ban- dan- nas.
col - ours of peo - ple who smile and shake hands and say 'Hel -lo!'

Words : David I. Arkin, b.1934

AS WE SING OF HOPE AND JOY 9.9. 10.10.

Elizabeth Alexander, b.1962

1.As we sing of__ hope and joy to - day, some know on - ly__ ang - uish and des - pair. How can we lift our voi - ces in this way, while some have pain and__ mis - er - y to spare?

6 As we sing of hope and joy today

As we sing of hope and joy today,
some know only anguish and despair.
How can we lift our voices in this way
while some have pain and misery to spare?

If a crumbling world we would renew,
we must sing no ordinary song,
peals from a noisy gong will never do;
in every breath compassion must belong.

Let this song our greatest hopes contain:
laughter of a well-fed child its tune,
roofs over every heart-beat its refrain,
its harmony from peaceful cities hewn.

Sing of joy while hammering each nail.
Sing of hope while pulling every weed,
so shall we sing together and prevail;
may every Alleluia bear a seed.

Elizabeth Alexander b. 1962

SUNNY BANK 87.87.Iambic

Traditional English Melody
Arr. Martin Shaw

1.At Can - dle - mas let can - dles shine, the
dark and gloom to ba - nish; with cheer a - dorn the
house of God, that all our fear__ may van - ish.

7 At Candlemas let candles shine

At Candlemas let candles shine,
the dark and gloom to banish;
with cheer adorn the house of God,
that all our fear may vanish.

For here we find, to treasure well,
a gift that grows by giving:
the sharing of God's candlelight,
the light of love for living.

And such a light for every land,
as well as Judah's glory:
a child of God, Emmanuel,
illuminates God's story.

John Bunyan

"I shall light a candle of understanding in
thine heart which shall not be put out." Esdras 14.25

8 Be ours a religion

Thomas Benjamin, b.1940

Be ours a re-lig-ion which like sun-shine goes ev-'ry-where, its

tem-ple all space, its shrine the good heart, its creed all

truth, its ri - - tu-al works of_ love_

Words: Theodore Parker, 1810-1860

9 Be thou with us

Thomas Benjamin, b.1940

Be Thou with us, now and al-ways, now and al-ways, bless_____ ed be._____

Words: Daniel Budd, b.1951

Music © Thomas Benjamin 1995. Used by permision.
Words © Daniel Budd. Used by permission.

WOODLAND 77.77.

Thomas Benjamin, b.1940

1.Be that guide whom love sus - tains. Rise a - bove the
dai - ly strife: lift on high the— good you find.
Help to - heal the hurts of life.

10 Be that guide whom love sustains

Be that guide whom love sustains.
Rise above the daily strife:
lift on high the good you find.
Help to heal the hurts of life.

Be that helper nothing daunts –
doubt of friend or taunt of foe.
Ever strive for liberty.
Show the path that life should go.

Be that builder trusting good,
bitter though the test may be:
through all ages they are right,
though they build in agony.

Be that teacher faith directs.
Move beyond the old frontier:
though the frightened fear that faith,
be tomorrow's pioneer!

Carl G. Seaburg 1922-1998

Shelley Jackson Denham, b.1950

1.Bless - ed spi - rit of my life, give me strength through stress and strife; help me live with dig - ni - ty; let me know ser - en - i - ty. Fill me with a vi - sion, clear my mind of fear and con - fu - sion. When my thoughts flow rest - less - ly, let peace find a home in me.

Music © Shelley Jackson Denham 1987. Used by permission.

11 Blessed Spirit of my life

Blessed Spirit of my life,
give me strength through stress and strife;
help me live with dignity;
let me know serenity.
Fill me with a vision,
clear my mind of fear and confusion.
When my thoughts flow restlessly,
let peace find a home in me.

Spirit of great mystery,
hear the still, small voice in me.
Help me live my wordless creed
as I comfort those in need.
Fill me with compassion;
be the source of my intuition.
Then when life is done for me,
let love be my legacy.

Shelley Jackson Denham b. 1950

SACRAMENTAL

Don Meacham

Bread and wine are of the earth, God's good food by us re-fined.
What a re-lish do we taste when we sa-vour God's good food.

Jes-us said "Re-mem-ber me when at board you sit and eat with

friends and fam-'ly ga-thered in, ga-thered in com-mun-ion close."

Sa-cred is our flesh and blood. We are all com-posed of God.

rall

Sa-cred is our flesh and blood. We are all com-posed of God.

12 Bread and wine are of the earth

Bread and wine are of the earth,
God's good food by us refined.

What a relish do we taste
when we savour God's good food!

Jesus said 'Remember me
when at board you sit and eat

with your friends and family
gathered in communion close.'

Sacred is our flesh and blood.
We are all composed of God.

Peter Sampson b. 1938

THE ASH GROVE 12.11.12.11.D.

Welsh Traditional Melody

Note: Verse 2 requires at * two quaver Ds on the upbeat of the Da Capo section

13 Bring flowers to our altar

Bring flowers to our altar to show nature's beauty,
the harvest of goodness in earth, sky and sea.
Bring light to our altar to guide every nation
from hatred to love and to humanity.
Bring a dove to our altar its wings ever flying
in permanent quest for the peace all may share.
Bring bread to our altar the hungry supplying
and feeding the poor who depend on our care.

Bring hope to our altar in your gentle dreaming
of all the good things that will make your heart glad.
Bring love to our altar, a bright witness beaming
to all who are burdened, or lonely or sad.
Bring work to our altar to help every nation
and celebrate all that's already achieved.
Come yourself to our altar in true dedication
to all the ideals we in common believe.

Lena Baxter

Words © Lena Cockroft. Used by permission.

Carlton R.Young, b.1926

1.Bring ma - ny names, beau - ti - ful and good;
2.Strong mo - ther God, work - ing night and day,

cel - e-brate in par - a - ble and sto - ry, ho - li - ness in
plan - ning all the won - ders of cre - a - tion, set - ting each e -

glo - ry, liv - ing, lov - ing God: Hail and Ho -
qua - tion, gen - i - us at play: Hail and Ho -

vv 1-5

v.6

san - na, bring ma - ny names!
san - na, strong mo - ther God!

great, liv-ing God!

14 Bring many names

1st and 2nd verses are with the music

Warm father God,
hugging every child,
feeling all the strains of human living,
caring and forgiving
till we're reconciled:
Hail and Hosanna,
warm father God!

Old, aching God,
grey with endless care,
calmly piercing evil's new disguises,
glad of good surprises,
wiser than despair:
Hail and Hosanna,
old, aching God!

Young, growing God,
eager, on the move,
saying no to falsehood and unkindness,
crying out for justice
giving all you have:
Hail and Hosanna,
young, growing God!

Great, living God,
never fully known,
joyful darkness far beyond our seeing,
closer yet than breathing,
everlasting home:
Hail and Hosanna,
great, living God!

Brian Wren, b. 1936

SERVANT SONG 87.87. Trochaic

Richard Gillard, b.1953
Arr. Betty Pulkingham

15 Brother, Sister, let me serve you

Brother, Sister, let me serve you,
let me be as Christ to you;
pray that I may have the grace to
let you be my servant too.

We are pilgrims on a journey,
and companions on the road;
we are here to help each other
walk a mile and bear the load.

I will hold the Christ-light for you
in the night-time of your fear;
I will hold my hand out to you,
speak the peace you long to hear.

I will weep when you are weeping;
when you laugh I'll laugh with you;
I will share your joy and sorrow
till we've seen this journey through.

When we sing to God in heaven
we shall find such harmony,
born of all we've known together
of Christ's love and agony.

Brother, Sister, let me serve you,
let me be as Christ to you;
pray that I may have the grace to
let you be my servant too.

Richard A. M. Gillard b. 1953

STUTTGART 87.87.

Christian Friedrich Witt, 1660-1716

16 Captive voices cry for freedom

Captive voices cry for freedom,
arms pull bars that will not bend;
liberty - our priceless treasure -
we will cherish and defend.

Free to doubt and free to question,
free to seek and free to find;
let us celebrate our freedom,
free in spirit, free in mind.

Free our minds from narrow thinking,
free our hearts from prejudice;
fill our minds with hope and reason,
fill our hearts with joy and peace.

Free from bigotry and anger,
free from ignorance and fear;
humankind heed freedom's challenge,
speak, O Lord, and make us hear.

Free all troubled minds from torment,
bring them comfort and repose;
grant us also such a freedom
when our lives draw to their close.

Free from fear of separation,
unenlightened creeds proclaim
universal destination –
God of love, from whom we came.

Jonathan Feast d. 1994

REGENT SQUARE 87.87.87.

Henry Smart, 1813-1879

Note: This tune is printed at No. 146 a semitone higher in Bb Major.

17 Caring God, your watching o'er us

Caring God, your watching o'er us
keeps the world in loving care.
Caring God, your coming to us
greets the world and bids her fair.
Caring God, your moving forwards
shows us how your world to share.

Andrew McKean Hill b. 1942

STENKA RAZIN 87.87.D.

Traditional Russian Melody
Arr. David Dawson

1.Cel - e - brate the gift of laugh - ter, cel - e - brate the gift of fun!

cel - e - brate till ev -'ry raft - er ech - oes songs so gai - ly sung!

Put a - way all gloom and sad - ness, let there be no ling-'ring trace;

cel - e - brate life's joy and glad - ness with a smile on ev -'ry face!

18 Celebrate the gift of laughter

1st verse with the music

Cultivate the art of clowning,
seek the joy in midst of pain.
Smiling's easier than frowning,
seek the rainbow in the rain!
If we smile, whate'er befall us,
and folk speak of us as mad,
take no heed of what they call us –
rather happy be, than sad!

There is cause for celebration
all around — yes, all around.
Humour's built into creation –
into sight and into sound.
Life is full of fresh surprises –
gifts of laughter, gifts of fun.
All we need are ears and eyeses
to appreciate each one!

Glory to the Cosmic Comic,
source of laughter, source of fun,
who delights in heavenly frolic
with the planets, stars and sun.
In the joyous re-creation
coming with each new-born day,
let us live in quiet elation —
come what may – yes, come what may.

Francis Simons 1939-1993

SANDWICK 10.10.11.11.

David Dawson, b.1939

1.Col-our and fra - grance, mag - i - cal rhy - thm,
sweet chang -ing mu - sic will change us with them: life with-in
life, in - ner light gent - ly glow - ing, sure - ly you
seem to be God's_____ vi - sion grow - ing.

19 Colour and fragrance

Colour and fragrance, magical rhythm,
sweet changing music will change us with them:
life within life, inner light gently glowing,
surely you seem to be God's vision growing.

O starry heavens, worlds of all splendour,
suns without number, new life engender:
wheel in a wheel with the light brightly glowing,
moving in harmony, God's vision growing.

Hand full of pebbles, high mountain passes,
depths of the ocean, dew on the grasses:
great things and small, with the light gently glowing,
word of the wordless song, God's vision growing.

Delicate beings, lace wing and sparrow
in field and forest, clover and yarrow:
life greeting life with the light brightly glowing
none are too small to be God's vision growing.

In human eyes burn the soul of living,
Illumines altars of loving giving:
greeting, we meet, seeing light brightly glowing,
share in a greater life, God's vision growing.

Shaper of all things, to us you've given
our chance to keep here on earth, a heaven.
Moving in harmony, light gently glowing,
may we be, gratefully, God's vision growing.

Norbert F. Capek, 1870-1942 ET Paul and Anita Munk

GONFALON ROYAL L.M.

Percy Carter Buck, 1871-1947

20 Come, all who look to God today

Come, all who look to God today,
stretch out your hands, enlarge your mind,
together share the living way
where all who humbly seek will find.

Come, young and old of every faith,
bring all your treasures of prayer,
and seek the living Spirit's breath
to realise the truths we share.

Bring your traditions' richest store,
your hymns and rites and cherished creeds;
explore your visions, pray for more,
since God delights to meet fresh needs.

Come, trust in God and live in peace,
anticipate that final light
when strife and bigotry shall cease,
and faith be lost in praise and sight. Amen.

Richard G. Jones b.1926

LEWIS FOLK MELODY 87.87.D.

Traditional Melody
Arr. John L. Bell, b.1949

1. Come and find the qui - et cen - tre in the crowd - ed
find the room for hope to en - ter, find the space where

life we lead, clear the cha - os and the clut - ter,
we are freed:

clear our eyes, that we can see all the things that

real - ly mat - ter, be at peace, and sim - ply be.

Music © WGRG, Iona Community, Glasgow G2 3DH. Used by permission.

21 Come and find the quiet centre

Come and find the quiet centre
in the crowded life we lead,
find the room for hope to enter,
find the space where we are freed:
clear the chaos and the clutter,
clear our eyes, that we can see
all the things that really matter,
be at peace, and simply be.

Silence is a friend who claims us,
cools the heat and slows the pace;
God it is who speaks and names us,
knows our being, touches base,
making space within our thinking,
lifting shades to show the sun,
raising courage when we're shrinking,
finding scope for faith begun.

In the Spirit let us travel,
open to each other's pain;
let our lives and fears unravel,
celebrate the space we gain:
there's a place for deepest dreaming,
there's a time for heart to care;
in the Spirit's lively scheming
there is always room to spare.

Shirley Erena Murray b. 1931

WESTMINSTER ABBEY 87.87.87.

Henry Purcell, 1659-1695

1.Come strong God and walk be - side us from the start__ to
jour- ney's end; come and guide our fal - t'ring foot - steps
as a true__ and trus - ty friend. Walk with us as
our com - pan - ion and our lives at last tran - scend.

22 Come strong God

Come strong God and walk beside us
from the start to journey's end;
come and guide our faltering footsteps
as a true and trusty friend.
Walk with us as our companion
and our lives at last transcend.

Come kind God and sleep beside us
so you may dispel our fears;
come and live among our dwellings
as the drier of our tears.
Sleep with us through nights of sorrow
till the new bright dawn appears.

Come warm God, burn strong within us;
melt with fire our frozen hearts;
come and stir our minds and spirits
while in life we play our parts.
Burn within us bright and freely
as the artist of our art.

Glory strong God, glory kind God
and to warm God, glory be.
Glory unto your creation
and its swirling energy.
Glory unto all that's living
in your glorious liberty.

Andrew McKean Hill b. 1942

BUNESSAN 55.54.D.

Old Gaelic Melody

1.Come to a wed - ding, come to a bless - ing,
come on a day when hap - pi - ness sings!
Come rain or sun, come win - ter or sum - mer,
cel - e - brate love and all that it brings.

23 Come to a wedding

Come to a wedding, come to a blessing,
come on a day when happiness sings!
Come rain or sun, come winter or summer,
celebrate love and all that it brings.

Thanks for the love that holds us together,
parent and child, and lover and friend,
thanks to the God whose love is our centre,
source of compassion, knowing no end.

Love is the gift, and love is the giver,
love is the gold that makes the day shine,
love forgets self to care for the other,
love changes life from water to wine.

Come to this wedding, asking a blessing
for all the years that living will prove:
health of the body, health of the spirit,
now to you both we offer our love.

Shirley Erena Murray b. 1931

A ROSE IN WINTER

Carolyn McDade, b.1935
Arr. David Dawson

1.Come, sing a song with me, come, sing a song with me, come, sing a song with me, that I - might know your mind.___ And I'll___ bring you hope___ when hope is hard to find,___ and I'll___ bring a song of love and a rose in the win - ter time.___

Chorus

24 Come, sing a song with me

Come, sing a song with me,
come, sing a song with me,
come, sing a song with me,
that I might know your mind.
And I'll bring you hope when hope is hard to find,
and I'll bring a song of love and a rose in the winter time.

Come, dream a dream with me,
come, dream a dream with me,
come, dream a dream with me,
that I might know your mind.
And I'll bring you hope when hope is hard to find,
and I'll bring a song of love and a rose in the winter time.

Come, walk in rain with me,
come, walk in rain with me,
come, walk in rain with me,
that I might know your mind.
And I'll bring you hope when hope is hard to find,
and I'll bring a song of love and a rose in the winter time.

Come, share a rose with me,
come, share a rose with me,
come, share a rose with me,
that I might know your mind.
And I'll bring you hope when hope is hard to find,
and I'll bring a song of love and a rose in the winter time.

Carolyn McDade b. 1935

WEM IN LEIDENSTAGEN 65.65.

Friedrich Filitz, 1804-1860

25 Conscience guide our footsteps

Conscience guide our footsteps,
reason light our ways,
as we struggle forwards
through the moral maze.

Honour every person;
value what they choose.
Good people may differ
in their honest views.

Hold all, gracious Being,
firmly by your clasp.
Shelter and enfold us
gently in your grasp.

Andrew McKean Hill b. 1942

NEANDER 87.87.87.

J. Neander, 1650-1680

26 Dancing sweet heart

Dancing sweet heart, may your kindness
be to one another shown;
and when human hearts are aching
may true human love be known.
Sweet heart calm us. Sweet heart heal us.
Sweet heart let your love be grown.

Beating small heart in the bodies
of all living things on earth,
pumping life blood through their systems
until death, from day of birth.
Small heart cleanse us. Small heart feed us.
Small heart give us joy and mirth.

Pulsing great heart of the cosmos
beating in the depths of space,
keeping suns and planets turning
placing earth in rightful place.
Great heart warm us. Great heart keep us.
Great heart hold us in your grace.

Andrew McKean Hill b. 1942

WINTER MEDITATION 77.76.89.76.

Shelley Jackson Denham, b.1950

1.Dark of win - ter, soft and still, your qui-et calm sur- rounds me.

Let my thoughts go where they will, ease my mind pro- found -ly. And

then my soul will sing a song, a bless - ed song of love e - ter - nal.

Gen-tle dark - ness, soft and still, bring your qui - et to me.

27 Dark of winter, soft and still

Dark of winter, soft and still,
your quiet calm surrounds me.
Let my thoughts go where they will,
ease my mind profoundly.
And then my soul will sing a song,
a blessed song of love eternal.
Gentle darkness, soft and still,
bring your quiet to me.

Darkness, soothe my weary eyes,
that I may see more clearly.
When my heart with sorrow cries,
comfort and caress me.
And then my soul may hear a voice,
a still, small voice of love eternal.
Darkness, when my fears arise,
let your peace flow through me.

Shelley Jackson Denham b. 1950

LOBT GOTT, IHR CHRISTEN 86.886.

Nikolaus Herman, 1480-1561
Harm. by J. S. Bach, 1685-1750

1.Dear wea - ver of our lives' de - sign whose

pat - terns all o - bey, with skil - ful fing - ers

gent - ly_ guide the stur - - dy threads that

will_ sur - vive the tan - gle_ of our days.

28 Dear weaver of our lives' design

Dear weaver of our lives' design
whose patterns all obey,
with skilful fingers gently guide
the sturdy threads that will survive
the tangle of our days.

Take up the fabric of our lives
with hands that gently hold;
bind in the ragged edge that care
would sunder and that pain would tear,
and mend our rav'ling souls.

Let eyes that in the plainest cloth
a hidden beauty see;
discern in us our richest hues,
show us the patterns we may use
to set our spirits free.

Nancy C. Dorian b. 1936

COE FEN C.M.D.

Ken Naylor, 1931-1991

1.Deep in the sha - dows of the past, far out from
set - tled lands, some no - mads tra - velled with their God a -
cross the de - sert sands. The dawn of hope for hu - man
kind by them was sensed and shown:_____ a pro - mise
call - ing them a - head, a fu - ture yet__ un - known.

29 Deep in the shadows of the past

1st verse is with the music

While others bowed to changeless gods,
they met a mystery:
God with an uncompleted name,
"I am what I will be",
and by their tents, around their fires,
in story, song and law,
they praised, remembered, handed on
a past that promised more.

From Exodus to Pentecost
the promise changed and grew,
while some, remembering the past,
recorded what they knew,
and some, in letters or laments,
in prophecy and praise,
recovered, held, and expressed
new hope for changing days.

For all the writings that survived,
for leaders long ago,
who sifted, copied and preserved
the Bible that we know,
give thanks, and find its story yet
our promise, strength and call,
the model of emerging faith,
alive with hope for all.

Brian Wren b. 1936

MIDDLETON 87.66.85.

David Dawson, b.1939

1.Each seek- ing faith is seek - ing light, and light dawns on our seek - ing, when clash -ing tongues com -bine to pray that light will shine, and guide and ga - ther all on earth in peace-ful greet - ing.

30 Each seeking faith is seeking light

Each seeking faith is seeking light,
and light dawns on our seeking,
when clashing tongues combine
to pray that light will shine,
and guide and gather all on earth
in peaceful greeting.

Each seeking faith is seeking truth,
for truth is lived by seeking,
and though our faiths conflict,
no dogma can restrict
the power of truth set free on earth
in honest meeting.

Each loving faith is seeking peace,
and peace is made by seeking
to spin the strands of trust
in patterns free and just,
till every family on earth
is in safe keeping.

Each living faith is seeking life,
and life flows through our seeking
to treasure, feel and show
the heart of what we know.
In every faith the Light, the Life,
is shining, speaking.

Brian Wren b. 1936

ABBOT'S LEIGH 87.87. D.

Cyril Vincent Taylor, 1907-1991

31 Earth is gift of God's creation

Earth is gift of God's creation,
ours to nurture or neglect.
We are called to witness boldly
that all life deserves respect.
We are kin to every being,
sharing space on earth, our home.
Yet we squander vast resources,
seek to save ourselves alone.

When our lifestyle lessens others
we become a measure less.
When we choose to live more simply
we confirm what we profess.
Can we lose our tunnel vision,
see those who are cast aside,
sense the hurt of broken pledges,
hear the planet's silent cries?

Tending space within earth's garden,
honouring the future here,
we can serve with God as partners,
a community of care.
Strengthened by the rainbow's promise,
sign of God's enduring grace,
let us dare to live our calling
in our time and in our place!

Edith Sinclair Downing 2000

Rowland Hugh Prichard, 1811-1887

32 Earth was given as a garden

Earth was given as a garden,
cradle for humanity;
tree of life and tree of knowledge
placed for our discovery.
Here was home for all your creatures
born of land and sky and sea;
all created in your image,
all to live in harmony.

Show to us again the garden
where all life flows fresh and free.
Gently guide your sons and daughters
into full maturity.
Teach us how to trust each other,
how to use for good our power,
how to touch the earth with reverence.
Then once more will Eden flower.

Bless the earth and all your children.
One creation, make us whole,
interwoven, all connected,
planet wide and inmost soul.
Holy mother, life bestowing,
bid our waste and warfare cease.
Fill us all with grace o'erflowing.
Teach us how to live in peace.

Roberta Bard b. 1940

REJOICE 7.7.8.7.

Louise Ruspini

1.En - ter, re - joice, and come in.

En - ter, re - joice, and come in._____ To-day will be a

joy - ful day;_____ en - ter, re - joice, and come in.

33 Enter, rejoice, and come in

Enter, rejoice, and come in.
Enter, rejoice, and come in.
Today will be a joyful day;
enter, rejoice, and come in.

Open your ears to the song.
Open your ears to the song.
Today will be a joyful day;
enter, rejoice, and come in.

Open your hearts everyone.
Open your hearts everyone.
Today will be a joyful day;
enter, rejoice, and come in.

Don't be afraid of some change.
Don't be afraid of some change.
Today will be a joyful day;
enter, rejoice, and come in.

Enter, rejoice, and come in.
Enter, rejoice, and come in.
Today will be a joyful day;
enter, rejoice, and come in.

Louise Ruspini

Words © Louise Ruspini from her book *Journey to Freedom*

LOBT DEN HERRN 87. 87.

J.F.Naue's:
Allgemeines Evangelisches Choralbuch, 1829

1.Far too long, by fear di - vi - ded, we have set - tled
with the sword quar - rels which should be de - ci - ded
by the re - con - cil - ing word.

34 Far too long, by fear divided

Far too long, by fear divided,
we have settled with the sword
quarrels which should be decided
by the reconciling word.

Now the nations are united,
though as yet in name alone,
and the distant goal is sighted
which the prophet souls have shown.

May, at last, we cease from warring,
barriers of hate remove;
and, earth's riches freely sharing,
found the dynasty of love.

John Andrew Storey, 1935–1997

Words © Sylvia Storey. Used by permission.

SIGISMUND 87.87.87.7.

Transylvanian Hymn Melody
Harmony by Larry Phillips, b.1948

1.Find a still-ness, hold a still-ness, let the still-ness car-ry me.

Find the si-lence, hold the si-lence, let the si-lence car-ry me.

In the spi-rit, by the spi-rit, with the spi-rit

giv-ing pow-er, I will find true har-mo-ny.

35 Find a stillness

Find a stillness, hold a stillness,
let the stillness carry me.
Find the silence, hold the silence,
let the silence carry me.
In the spirit, by the spirit,
with the spirit giving power,
I will find true harmony.

Seek the essence, hold the essence,
let the essence carry me.
Let me flower, help me flower,
watch me flower, carry me.
In the spirit, by the spirit,
with the spirit giving power,
I will find true harmony.

Carl G. Seaburg 1922-1998
based on a Transylvanian Unitarian text

36 For everyone born

A PLACE AT THE TABLE 11.10 11.10.+ Refrain   Lauri True, b.1961

1.For ev'-ry-one born, a place at the ta - ble, for
2.For wo-man and man, a place at the ta - ble, re-
3.For young and for old, a place at the ta - ble, a
4.For just and un - just, a place at the ta - ble, a-
5.For ev' - ry one born, a place at the ta - ble, to

ev' - ry - one born, clean wa - ter and bread,_____
vis - ing the role, de - cid - ing the share_____
voice to be heard, a part in the song,_____
bu - ser, a - bused, with need to for give,_____
live with - out fear, and sim - ply to be,_____

— a shel - ter, a space, a safe place for grow-
— with wis - dom and grace, di - vid - ing the pow-
— the hands of a child in hands kind and wrink-
— in an - ger in hurt, a mind - set of mer-
— to work, to speak out, to wit - ness and wor-

Words: *Shirley E Murray*

37 For the fruits of all creation

ADELPHI 84.84.888.4.

Alan Williams

1.For the fruits of all cre - a - tion, thanks be to God;
ward of la -bour, God's will is done;
of the spi- rit, thanks be to God;

for the gifts to ev - 'ry na - tion, thanks be to God;
in the help we give our neigh- bour, God's will is done;
for the good we all in - her - it, thanks be to God;

for the plough- ing, sow - ing, reap_ ing,
in the world - wide task of - ca - ring
for the won - ders that as - tound - us,

Words: *Frederick Pratt Green, 1903-2000*

MILE HIGH 87.87.D.

Larry Harris

Unison

1.For the mu - sic of cre - a - tion, for the song your spi - rit sings,

for your sound's di - vine ex - press - ion, burst of joy in liv - ing things;

God, our God, the world's com - po - ser, hear us, ech-oes of your voice.

Mus - ic is your art, your glo - ry, let the hu - man heart re - joice.

38 For the music of creation

For the music of creation,
for the song your spirit sings,
for your sound's divine expression,
burst of joy in living things;
God, our God, the world's composer,
hear us, echoes of your voice.
Music is your art, your glory,
let the human heart rejoice.

Psalms and symphonies exalt you,
drum and trumpet, string and reed,
simple melodies acclaim you,
tunes that rise from deepest need;
hymns of longing and belonging,
carols from a cheerful throat,
lilt of lullaby and love song
catching heaven in a note.

All the voices of the ages
in transcendent chorus meet,
worship lifting up the senses,
hands that praise and dancing feet;
over discord and diversion
music speaks your joy and peace,
harmony of earth and heaven,
song of God that cannot cease!

Shirley Erena Murray b. 1931

THAXTED

Gustav Holst, 1874 - 1934
Arr. David Dawson

39 For the splendour of creation

For the splendour of creation that draws us to inquire,
for the mystery of knowledge to which our hearts aspire,
for the deep and subtle beauties which delight the eye and ear,
for the discipline of logic, the struggle to be clear,
for the unexplained remainder, the puzzling and the odd:
for the joy and pain of learning, we give you thanks, O God.

For the scholars past and present whose bounty we digest,
for the teachers who inspire us to summon forth our best,
for our rivals and companions, sometimes foolish, sometimes
(wise,
for the human web upholding this noble enterprise,
for the common life that binds us through days that soar or plod:
for this place and for these people, we give you thanks, O God.

Carl Pickens Daw Jr. b. 1944

FOR YOU SHALL GO OUT

Thomas Benjamin, b.1940

40 For you shall go out in joy

For you shall go out in joy,
for you shall go out in joy,
    and come back in peace,
    and come back in peace,
      blessed be.

adapted from Isaiah 55

BRIDEGROOM 87.87.6.

Peter Cutts, b.1937

Unison

1.From the crush of wealth and pow - er, some - thing bro - ken in us all, waits the spi - rit's si - lent hour__ plead - ing with a poi - gnant call, bind__ all my wounds__ a - gain.

41 From the crush of wealth and power

From the crush of wealth and power,
something broken in us all,
waits the spirit's silent hour
pleading with a poignant call,
bind all my wounds again.

Even now our hearts are wary
of the friend we need so much.
When I see the pain you carry,
shall I, with a gentle touch,
bind all your wounds again?

When our love for one another
makes our burdens light to bear,
find the sister and the brother,
hungry for the feast we share;
bind all their wounds again.

Every time our spirits languish
terrified to draw too near,
may we know each other's anguish
and, with love that casts out fear,
bind all our wounds again.

Kendyl L. R. Gibbons b. 1955

42 From the light of days remembered

THE FIRE OF COMMITMENT

Jason Shelton, b.1972

1.From the light of days re - mem - bered burns a
2.From the sto - ries of our liv - ing rings a
3.From the dreams of youth - ful vi - sion comes a

bea - con bright and clear, guid - ing hands and hearts and
song both brave and free, call - ing pil - grims still to
new, pro - phe - tic voice, which de- mands a deep - er

spi - rits in - to faith set free from fear.
wit - ness to the life of lib - er - ty. When the
jus - tice built by our cour - a - geous choice.

fire of com-mit-ment sets our mind and soul a-blaze; when our hun-ger and our pas-sion meet to call us on our way; when we live with deep as-sur-ance of the flame that burns with-in, then our pro-mise finds ful-fil-ment and our fu-ture can be-gin.

Words: Jason Shelton and Mary Katherine Morn

Music and Words © 2001. Used by permission.

43 Gather the spirit

Jim Scott, b.1945

1.Ga - ther the spi - rit, har - vest the power. Our sep -'rate
2.Ga - ther the spi - rit of heart and mind. Seeds for the
3.Ga - ther the spi - rit grow - ing in all, drawn by the

fires will kin - dle one flame. Wit - ness the mys - ter -
sow - ing are laid in store. Nur - tured in love and
moon and fed by the sun. Win - ter to spring, and

y of this hour. Our trials in this light ap-pear all the
con -science re - fined, with bo - dy and spi - rit u - ni - ted once
sum - mer to fall, the chor-us of life re- sound- ing as

92

Words: Jim Scott, b.1945

Words and Music © Jim Scott, PO Box 4025, Shrewsbury MA 01545-7025
www.jimscottmusic.com Used by permission.

SINE NOMINE 10.10.10.4.

Ralph Vaughan Williams, 1872-1958

44 Give thanks for life

Give thanks for life, the measure of our days,
mortal, we pass through beauty that decays,
yet sing to God our hope, our love, our praise:
Alleluia, Alleluia!

Give thanks for those whose lives shone with a light
caught from the Christ-flame, gleaming through the night,
who touched the truth, who burned for what is right:
Alleluia, Alleluia!

Give thanks for all, our living and our dead,
thanks for the love by which our life is fed,
a love not changed by time or death or dread:
Alleluia, Alleluia!

Give thanks for hope that like a seed of grain
lying in darkness, does its life retain
to rise in glory, growing green again:
Alleluia, Alleluia!

Shirley Erena Murray b. 1931

GO IN PEACE

Natalie Sleeth, b.1930

Note. May be sung in a number of ways: unaccompanied, as a round - with or without the left hand accompaniment. The chords are given for improvised keyboard or guitar accompaniment - this will not work with the given left hand part.

45 Go now in peace

Go now in peace.
Go now in peace.
May the love of God surround you everywhere,
everywhere you may go.

Natalie Allyn Sleeth Wakely 1930-1992 based on Luke 2:29

46 Go your way in peace

Mozart - Clarinet Concerto, K.622.
Adapted by Jim Scott, b.1945

1.Go   your way in   peace.   Wan - der as you   may.
2.Bright and brave the dreams   born in dark-est night.

Bless -ed   is the path you take. May love guide you on your   way.
Mind - ful make our ev- 'ry step, hon - our all with - in our   sight.

Part 2

Com-fort find in truth.
Minds and hearts now one,

May your strug-gles
'til we meet a-

Part 1

Com-fort find in truth.
Minds and hearts now one,

May your strug-gles cease.
'til we meet a - gain.

cease. May the fire with-in your heart light the way of peace.
gain. Hold the vi-sion of our peace sa-cred un-til then.

May the fire with-in your heart light the way of peace.
Hold the vi-sion of our peace sac-red un-til then.

Words: Jim Scott, b.1945

FYNN VALLEY 85.85.

Robert Waller

47 God around us, God within us

God around us, God within us,
God the heart of all;
God, we praise you; God we thank you;
God, we hear your call.

You want us to love each other,
you want us to be
caring neighbours, sisters, brothers,
blessed with amity.

You would have us be good stewards
of this living earth;
caring for its lands and oceans,
all they bring to birth.

You have sent us saints and prophets,
gentle avatars;
still your spirit speaks in Jesus,
sings among the stars.

God above us, God between us,
God who makes us one,
calling us to be compassion,
may your will be done.

Clifford Martin Reed b. 1947

Words © Clifford Martin Reed, 2009. Used with pemission.

48 God of creation

MACCABAEUS 10.11.11.11. + Refrain

George Frederick Handel, 1685-1759
from *Judas Maccabaeus*

1.God of cre - a - tion, pri - mal fi - nal one;

through our trans-form - a - tion let thy will be done.

Firm a - gainst temp -ta - tion, mod - est in the sun,

may each soul and na - tion see thy task be - gun.

Refrain

God of cre - a - tion, pri - mal fi - nal one;

through our trans-form-a - tion   let thy will be done.

1st verse is printed with the music

Far do we seek thee,
rarely understand
how through pain and folly
speaks the great command.
When we cry against thee,
fear thy forming hand,
light us through the valley
to the promised land.
> *God of creation,*
> *primal, final one;*
> *through our transformation*
> *let thy will be done.*

God of our growing,
pure and perfect seed,
fructify our knowing,
glorify our deed.
Set our purpose flowing
free from hate and greed,
still with thy bestowing
all our human need.
> *God of creation,*
> *primal, final one;*
> *through our transformation*
> *let thy will be done.*

Words: Mary Boynton Parke

JOEL(1) 87.87.D.

Sally Ann Morris, b.1952

1.God of day and God of dark-ness, now we stand be-fore the night;

as the shad-ows stretch and deep-en, come and make our dark-ness bright.

All cre-a - tion still is groan-ing for the dawn-ing of your might,

when the sun of peace and jus-tice fills the earth with ra - diant light.

49 God of day and God of darkness

God of day and God of darkness,
now we stand before the night;
as the shadows stretch and deepen,
come and make our darkness bright.
All creation still is groaning
for the dawning of your might,
when the sun of peace and justice
fills the earth with radiant light.

Praise to you in day and darkness,
you our source and you our end;
praise to you who love and nurture us
as a father, mother, friend.
Grant us all a peaceful resting,
let each mind and body mend,
let us rise refreshed tomorrow
for the tasks which you will send.

Marty Haughen b. 1950

Welsh Traditional Melody

1.God of ev - 'ry stone and peb - ble, gran - ite moun - tain,
shift - ing sand, ti - ny stream and migh - ty oc - ean,
de - serts and the fruit - ful land. Ev - 'ry cloud__ and
ev - 'ry rain - drop speaks the work - ing of your hand.

50 God of every stone and pebble

1st verse is with the music

God of grass, of beech and oak tree,
of the sweet fruit and the sour,
all the grain that feeds the hungry,
every lovely herb and flower;
leaves of every shape and colour
show the working of your power.

God of every living creature,
each so marvellously designed,
some to roam in glorious freedom,
some in service to our kind;
teach us ever to remember
all are workings of your mind.

God of words and worlds of wonder
brought to us in gifts of art,
painting, building, joy of music,
all where beauty plays a part
for our pleasure or our learning;
these are workings of your heart.,

God of all that love your treasures,
deepest mines to stars above,
may we learn your works to cherish,
just and faithful stewards prove;
and by caring, praying, sharing
show the working of your love.

Barbara S. Russell

BARDEN 87.87.D.

David Dawson, b.1939

1. God of grace and God of laugh-ter,_____ sing-ing worlds from nought to be; sun and stars and all there - af - ter_____ joined in cos - mic har - mo - ny, giv-ing songs of joy and won -der,_____ mus-ic ma - king hearts re - joice; let our prais - es swell like thun-der_____ ech - o - ing our Ma - ker's voice.

51 God of grace and God of laughter

God of grace and God of laughter,
singing worlds from nought to be;
sun and stars and all thereafter
joined in cosmic harmony,
giving songs of joy and wonder,
music making hearts rejoice;
let our praises swell like thunder
echoing our Maker's voice.

When our lives are torn by sadness
heal our lives with tuneful balm;
when all seems discordant madness
help us find a measured calm.
Steady us with music's anchor
when the storms of life increase;
in the midst of hurt and rancour,
make us instruments of peace.

Turn our sighing into singing,
music born of hope restored;
set our souls and voices ringing,
tune our hearts in true accord
till we form a mighty chorus
joining angel choirs above
with all those who went before us
in eternal hymns of love.

Carl Pickens Daw Jr. b. 1944

MANY NAMES 55. 88.D. + Refrain

William P. Rowan, b.1951

1.God of ma - ny Names, ga - thered in - to One,
God of Hov -'ring Wings, Womb and Birth of time,

in your glo-ry come and meet us, mov-ing, end - less-ly Be-com-ing:
joy- ful -ly we sing your prais- es, Breath of life in ev-'ry peo - ple,

Refrain

Hush, hush, hal - le - lu - ia, hal - le - lu - ia! Shout, shout, hal - le-

lu - ia, hal - le - lu - ia! Sing, sing, hal-le - lu - ia, hal - le - lu -

1.2. | 3.

ia! Sing, God is love,__ God is love! love!

52 God of many names

God of many Names,
gathered into One,
in your glory come and meet us,
moving, endlessly Becoming:
God of Hovering Wings,
Womb and Birth of time,
joyfully we sing your praises,
Breath of life in every people—
  Hush, hush, halleluia, halleluia!
  Shout, shout, halleluia, halleluia!
  Sing, sing, halleluia, halleluia!
  Sing God is love, God is love!

God of Jewish faith,
Exodus and Law,
in your glory come and meet us,
joy of Miriam and Moses:
God of Jesus Christ,
Rabbi of the poor,
joyfully we sing your praises,
crucified, alive for ever —
Refrain

God of Wounded Hands,
Web and Loom of love,
in your glory come and meet us,
Carpenter of new creation;
God of many Names
gathered into One,
joyfully we sing your praises,
Moving, endlessly Becoming —
Refrain

Brian Wren, b. 1936

BUNESSAN 55.54.D.

Gaelic Traditional Melody
Harm. David Evans, 1874-1948

53 God, the All-Holy

God, the All-Holy,
Maker and Mother,
gladly we gather,
bringing in prayer
old hurts for healing,
new hopes for holding,
giving, receiving,
loving and care.

Spirit, All-Seeing,
knitting and blending
joy in desiring
friendship and ease,
make our belonging
loyal and lasting,
so that our pledging
freshens and frees.

Christ, All-Completing,
Nature enfolding,
evil exhausting
in love's embrace,
weaving and mending
make every ending
God's new beginning
glowing with grace.

Brian Wren, b. 1936

EMPATHY 6.4.8.10.

Ian P. Render, b.1954

1.God weeps at love with-held, at strength mis-used,
at child-ren's in-no-cence a - bused,_____ and, till we
change the way we love, God
weeps._____

Music © Ian P. Render. Used by permission.

54 God weeps

God weeps
> at love withheld,
> at strength misused,
> at children's innocence abused,
and, till we change the way we love,
> God weeps.

God bleeds
> at anger's fist,
> at trust betrayed,
> at women battered and afraid,
and, till we change the way we win,
> God bleeds.

God cries
> at hungry mouths,
> at running sores,
> at creatures dying without cause,
and, till we change the way we care,
> God cries.

God waits
> for stones to melt,
> for peace to seed,
> for hearts to hold each other's need,
and till we understand the Christ,
> God waits.

Shirley Erena Murray b. 1931

FRANCIS DAVID 77.66.7.

Transylvanian Hymn, 1607
Harmony: Larry Phillips, b.1948

1.God who fills the un - i - verse from the a - tom
to the stars, make firm my change -ful heart so I may
do my part and bring joy to all the earth.

Music © Unitarian Universalist Association (Singing the Living Tradition).

55 God who fills the universe

God who fills the universe
from the atom to the stars,
make firm my changeful heart
so I may do my part
and bring joy to all the earth.

God who webs the universe
with amazing mysteries,
make glad my fragile soul
so I can see life whole
and bring hope to all on earth.

God who keeps the universe
by the truths of living love,
make strong that love in me
so I can set it free
and bring peace to all on earth.

Carl G. Seaburg 1922-1998

HOLY MANNA 87.87.D.

Melody from *The Southern Harmony*, 1855
Arr. David Dawson

1. God, who stretched the span-gled hea-vens, in-fin-ite in
   flung the suns in burn-ing ra di-ance through the si-lent

time and place,
fields of space,
we your child-ren, in your like-ness

share in-ven-tive pow'rs with you. Great Cre-a-tor,

still cre-a-ting show us what we yet may do.

56 God, who stretched

1st verse is with the music

Proudly rise our modern cities,
stately buildings, row on row;
yet their windows, blank, unfeeling,
stare on canyoned streets below,
where the lonely drift unnoticed
in the city's ebb and flow,
lost to purpose and to meaning,
scarcely caring where they go.

We have ventured worlds undreamed of
since the childhood of our race;
known the ecstasy of winging
through untravelled realms of space;
probed the secrets of the atom,
yielding unimagined power,
facing us with life's destruction
at our most triumphal hour.

As each far horizon beckons,
may it challenge us anew,
children of creative purpose,
serving others, honouring you.
May our dreams prove rich with promise,
each endeavour, well begun.
Great Creator, give us guidance
till our goals and yours are one.

Catherine Cameron b. 1927

ST. SAVIOUR C.M.

Frederick George Baker, 1821-77

57 God, you have given us power

God, you have given us power to sound
depths hitherto unknown:
to probe earth's hidden mysteries,
and make their might our own.

Great are your gifts: yet greater far
this gift, O God, bestow,
that as to knowledge we attain
we may in wisdom grow.

Let wisdom's godly fear dispel
all fears that hate imparts;
give understanding to the mind,
and, with new minds, new hearts.

O for your glory and our good
may we your gifts employ,
lest, maddened by the lust of power,
we shall ourselves destroy.

G. W. Briggs 1875-1959 altered

PICARDY 87.87.11.7.   French Traditional Melody

1.Grant us, God, a mind to__ know you, let us feel you stir in our hearts; fill our lives with your a - bun - dance show us how to play our - parts. In this chang- ing world, in which we make our way, keep us in your love ev - er true.

58 Grant us, God, a mind to know you

Grant us, God, a mind to know you,
let us feel you stir in our hearts;
fill our lives with your abundance
show us how to play our parts.
In this changing world, in which we make our way,
keep us in your love ever true.

Help us to be kind to each other,
value people's thoughts and needs.
Human hearts can give so much loving,
human flesh for mercy pleads.
In this warring world in which we would survive
why should we not give peace a chance?

Keep our spirits young and lively,
teach our children how to flower.
When our limbs begin to weaken
send your comfort, let us know your power.
In this jostling world in which we strain and strive
let us hear your still small voice.

Peter Sampson b. 1938

AVE VIRGO VIRGINUM 77.77.+Alleluias

Melody from
Johann Horn's Gesangbuch, 1544

1.Ground, it's time for your re - birth, Al_____ le - lu - ia!
Flow'r and leaf buds blos- som forth, Al_____ le - lu - ia!

Rise from soil, rise from the ground, Al_____ le - lu - ia!

Now that spring is all a- round, Al_____ le - lu - ia!

59 Ground, it's time for your rebirth

Ground, it's time for your rebirth, Alleluia!
Flower and leaf buds blossom forth, Alleluia!
Rise from soil, rise from the ground, Alleluia!
Now that spring is all around, Alleluia!

Friend, take heart and find new cheer, Alleluia!
Your new birth at last is here, Alleluia!
Rise above despair, defeat, Alleluia!
Now with joy your new life greet, Alleluia!

Earth, for you there is new scope, Alleluia!
New life, new world and new hope, Alleluia!
Rise from travail into light, Alleluia!
Now that we have seen what's right, Alleluia!

Cosmos, broad and deep with space, Alleluia!
Stars and planets you embrace, Alleluia!
Raise us to our human part, Alleluia!
Hold us with your loving heart, Alleluia!

Andrew McKean Hill b. 1942

THIS OLD MAN

Traditional
Arr. David Dawson

Note: This is a very simple tune. The semitone 'shifts' add some interest, but you can, if you wish, play all seven verses in the same key. Guitarists may find the Db Major section difficult - adapt as necessary.

60 Here I am, all alone

Here I am, all alone,
can't do this job on my own;
but if you come with me, it'll soon be done –
two can do much more than one!

Here we are, just us two;
there is still so much to do,
but if you can join us, then there will be three:
we can do it – just you see!

One plus two, making three,
work together happily,
but for some things we need just a little more;
can you come and make it four?

Can you see four of us
get things done without a fuss?
But we sometimes meet things bigger than they seem;
five of us will make a team!

Watch us work, famous five,
we're the finest five alive,
till we find some things we're never going to lift;
two more hands will make them shift!

Counting up, now we're six;
see what we can fetch and fix,
but there's always room for many, many more –
seven, eight, nine, ten, or a score!

Jesus called twelve to start,
hundreds, thousands, play a part –
if the work is worth it, getting anywhere,
everyone can take a share!

Christopher Idle

LOVE UNKNOWN 66.66.88.

John Ireland, 1879-1962

Unison

1. Here in this moment's song great symphonies are sung; all people we contain, ageless, though old____ or young: in passing words and melody we celebrate eternity.

61 Here in this moment's song

Here in this moment's song
great symphonies are sung;
all people we contain,
ageless, though old or young:
in passing words and melody
we celebrate eternity.

Thus, in each moment small
we can contain all hours;
in everyone the All
expresses and empowers;
each person great, a living world
from whom uniqueness is unfurled.

Hope shall admit no bounds,
as love no limit knows;
each new-born dream made real
in our commitment grows;
the possible, the yet-to-be
is now, is here, is you and me.

Frank R. Clabburn 1947-2000

Words © : Sheila Clabburn. Used by permission.

OLD 124TH 10.10.10.10.10.

Genevan Psalter, 1551

62 Here we have gathered

Here we have gathered, gathered side by side;
circle of kinship, come and step inside!
May all who seek here find a kindly word;
may all who speak here feel they have been heard.
Sing now together this, our hearts' own song.

Here we have gathered, called to celebrate
days of our lifetime, matters small and great:
we of all ages, women, children, men,
infants and sages, sharing what we can.
Sing now together this, our hearts' own song.

Life has its battles, sorrows, and regret:
but in the shadows, let us not forget:
we who now gather know each other's pain;
kindness can heal us: as we give, we gain.
Sing now in friendship this, our hearts' own song.

Alicia S. Carpenter b. 1930

AU CLAIR DE LA LUNE 11.11.11.11.

French Traditional Melody
Arr. David Dawson

1.Hope is born in spring - time though the cold wind chills;

hope as strong as snow - drops, gold as daf - fo - dils.

Hope be in our plant - ing, hope be in our prayer,

be the key that op - ens hearts to greet the year.

Music © Arrangement used by permission.

63 Hope is born in springtime

Hope is born in springtime though the cold wind chills;
hope as strong as snowdrops, gold as daffodils.
Hope be in our planting, hope be in our prayer,
be the key that opens hearts to greet the year.

Summer bids us welcome, strong and brave and bright;
warms us with her sunshine, cheers us with her light.
Sudden storm, then silence; feel the pulse of power;
everywhere around her, springtime buds in flower.

Autumn's golden glory seems to hold the sun;
singing through the cornfields "Look what God has done –
ripened field and fruit trees, filled your barns with grain,
seeds for next year's sowing harvested again."

Patient winter teaches we must sometimes pause;
listen to the silence, learn the living laws.
Gather strength in quietness, ponder nature's ways;
still our souls with praying, lift our hearts with praise.

Though the years may bring us sadness, gladness, strife;
birth and growth and living make the joys of life.
Count the many blessings of our daily lives;
then, through joy and sorrow, all that's good survives.

Barbara S. Russell

WENTWORTH 55.55.

Peter Cutts, b.1937

1.How can we con - fine God____ with - in our mind, held____

____ with - in a creed____ hu - man - ly de - signed?

Music © 2002 Stainer & Bell Ltd, 23 Gruneisen Road, London N3 1DZ. www.stainer.co.uk

64 How can we confine

How can we confine
God within our mind,
held within a creed
humanly designed?

How can we be sure
that the way we know
is the only path
that this God might show?

Surely such a joy
cannot be contained
by a single plan,
humanly explained?

People of all faiths,
let us all conspire;
source and ground of life,
answer our desire.

As we long to know
answers to our plight,
take us, lead our quest,
dancing to the light.

Andrew Pratt b. 1948

ST. STEPHEN C.M.

William Jones, 1726-1800

65 How good it is, what pleasure comes

How good it is, what pleasure comes,
when people live as one.
When peace and justice light the way
the will of God is done.

True friendship then like fragrant oil
surrounds us with delight;
and blessings shine like morning dew
upon the mountain height.

How good it is when walls of fear
come tumbling to the ground.
When arms are changed to farming tools
the fruits of life abound.

What quiet joy can bloom and grow
when people work for peace,
when hands and voices join as one
that hate and war may cease.

Ruth C. Duck b. 1947 [from Psalm 133]

NESFIELD 886.D.

David Dawson, b.1939

1.How won-der-ful this world of thine, a frag-ment of a fi - 'ry sun, how love - ly and how small, where all things serve thy great de - sign, where life's ad-ven-ture is be - gun in God, the life of all.

Music © David Dawson 2009. Used by permission.

66 How wonderful this world of thine

How wonderful this world of thine,
a fragment of a fiery sun,
how lovely and how small,
where all things serve thy great design,
where life's adventure is begun
in God, the life of all.

The smallest seed in secret grows,
and thrusting upward answers soon
the bidding of the light;
the bud unfurls into a rose;
the wings within the whole cocoon
are perfected for flight.

The migrant bird in winter fled,
shall come again with spring, and build
in this same shady tree;
by secret wisdom surely led,
homeward across the clover field
hurries the honey bee.

O thou, whose greater gifts are ours -
a conscious will, a thinking mind,
a heart to worship thee -
O take these strange unfolding powers,
and teach us through thy Word to find
the life more full and free.

Frederick Pratt Green, 1903-2000

NIAGARA L.M.

Robert Jackson, 1842-1914

67 I am that great and fiery force

I am that great and fiery force
sparkling in everything that lives,
in shining of the river's course,
in greening grass that glory gives.

I shine in glitter on the seas,
in burning sun, in moon and stars.
In unseen wind, in verdant trees
I breathe within, both near and far.

And where I breathe there is no death,
and meadows glow with beauties rife.
I am in all the spirit's breath,
the thundered word, for I am Life.

Hildegard of Bingen, 1098-1179 ET unknown 20th century

Words ET © Translator

STREETS OF LAREDO 12.12.12.12.

Traditional Melody
Arr. David Dawson

1.I dream of a church that joins in with God's laugh-ing_

as she rocks in her rap - ture, en - joy - ing her art:

she's glad of her world, in its risk - ing and grow - ing:

'tis the child she has borne and holds close to her heart.

68 I dream of a church

I dream of a church that joins in with God's laughing
as she rocks in her rapture, enjoying her art:
she's glad of her world, in its risking and growing:
'tis the child she has borne and holds close to her heart.

I dream of a church that joins in with God's weeping
as she crouches, weighed down by the sorrow she sees:
she cries for the hostile, the cold and no-hoping,
for she bears in herself our despair and dis-ease.

I dream of a church that joins in with God's dancing
as she moves like the wind and the wave and the fire:
a church that can pick up its skirts, pirouetting,
with the steps that can signal God's deepest desire.

I dream of a church that joins in with God's loving
as she bends to embrace the unlovely and lost,
a church that can free, by its sharing and daring,
the imprisoned and poor, and then shoulder the cost.

God, make us a church that joins in with your living,
as you cherish and challenge, rein in and release,
a church that is winsome, impassioned, inspiring;
lioness of your justice and lamb of your peace.

Kate Compston

69 I stand outside your door

CALEB 11.10.11.10.11.10.

Alan Williams

1. I stand out-side your door, will you ad-mit me? I have no home, no land, no friend, no life._____ I ask so lit-tle from your great a-bun-dance, a place to sleep, some food for child, for

heard a pro-mise from your dis-tant coun-try:____ a whis-per of your peace through sounds of war;_____ we travel-led long, re-jec-ted, cast a-sun-der, no rest we found, far from our na-tive

so we come and wait up-on your bor-ders:____ a-non-y-mous, for-sa-ken and a-lone._____ Where now your pro-mise? Where is love, com-pas-sion? Where now the hope? Has your heart turned to

wife.____ I have no pride, no plea, ex - cept 'a - sy____
shore.____ We had no pride, no plea, ex - cept 'a - sy____
stone?____ For - get your pride and hear our plea 'a - sy____

lum,'____ a place of peace, be - yond our world of
lum,'____ will you pro - vide for us an o - pen
lum,'____ and let us know one coun - try and one

|1.|2.|3.|

strife.____ 2.We -
door.____ — 3.And -
home.____ ____

Words: Frank R. Clabburn, 1947-2000

Music © Alan Williams. Used by permission.
Words © Sheila Clabburn. Used by permission.

70 I wish I knew how

Words and Music
Billy Taylor and Dick Dallas

MANDELA 11.11.11.12.12.

1.I wish I knew how____ it would feel____ to be free.__
2.I wish I could share____ all the love____ in my heart,__
3.I wish I could give____ all I'm long - ing to give.__
4.I wish I could be____ like a bird____ in the sky.__

_____ I wish I could break____ all these chains
_____ re - move all the bars____ that still keep
_____ I wish I could live____ like I'm long
_____ How sweet it would be____ if I found

---- hold- ing me.____ I wish I could say__ all the things
---- us a - part.____ I wish you could know__ what it means
---- ing to live.____ I wish I could do__ all the things
---- I could fly.____ I'd soar to the sun__ and look down

146

HYMN OF THE WIND

Myrna Michell, b.1951

1.If all of the pro-phets were si-lent,— and the gos-pel of law heard no more; if— ev-e-ry cov'nant was bro-ken, and ev-e-ry prom-ise ig-nored, we would still have full mea-sure of wor-ship,— we would have a full mea-sure and more____ in the hymn of the wind in the tree-tops__ and the prayer of the sea to the shore.

71 If all the prophets were silent

1st verse is with the music

For the night is a chalice of mercy
that the day must kneel humbly before
crying "Goddess forgive and preserve me"
and let me come in through the door.
Let the kiss of your wisdom complete me,
as I unpeel my pride and I pour
through the crack in the door into midnight,
through the crack in the midnight door.

O Father of sweetness and richness
lift up now our hearts to adore,
O Mother of strangeness and grace
now sing in our senses and soar.
O shine in our souls and please teach us
to be silent and tranquill before
the hymn of the wind in the treetops
and the prayer of the sea to the shore.

Then kneel down in peace and be joyful,
and rise up in praise to be sure
that the pure law of love shall prevail,
and the heavenly word shall endure.
As it was from the very beginning
and so it shall be evermore
in the hymn of the wind in the treetops
and the prayer of the sea to the shore.

Tom McCready

SOLL'S SEIN C.M.D.   Melody from Corner's *Geistliche Nachtigall*, 1658

1.If, as we come to one we love, we meet___ just
that look at us in ig - nor - ance and fail___ to

star-ing eyes
re - cog - nise,   how can we hold on to the love from

which___ our care de - rives? We ask, we plead, we

hope, we trust our love___ might still sur - vive.

72 If, as we come to one we love

If, as we come to one we love,
we meet just staring eyes
that look at us in ignorance
and fail to recognise,
how can we hold on to the love
from which our care derives?
We ask, we plead, we hope, we trust
our love might still survive.

If as we look to those who love,
dependent on their care,
we struggle, cannot speak their name,
inanimate we stare,
how can they still hold us in love
from which their care derives?
We ask, we plead, we hope, we trust
their love might still survive.

O God, we come to you in love
in doubt as much as faith,
with frail and faltering hands we grasp
the offer of your grace;
and can you recognise the ones
who barely know your name?
We ask, we plead, we hope, we trust
your love remains the same.

Andrew Pratt b. 1948

73 If every woman in the world

Karen MacKay, b.1952
Arr. Jerome Kyles, b.1974

1.If ev'ry wo- man in the world had her mind set on
man___ in the world had his mind set on
lea- der in the world shared a vi- sion of
na- tion in the world set a true course for

free- dom, if ev'ry wo- man in the world dreamed a sweet dream of
free- dom, if ev'ry bro- ther stood with bro -ther as a wit - ness for
free- dom, if ev'ry lea- der in the world shared a sweet dream of
free- dom, if ev'ry na - tion raised its child-ren in a cul - ture of

peace, if ev-'ry woman of ev-'ry na-tion, young and old, each gen-er
peace, if ev-'ry man___ of ev-'ry na-tion, young and old, each gen-er
peace, if ev-'ry lea-der of ev-'ry na-tion worked for jus-tice and lib-er
peace, if all our sons___ and all our daughters reached in friendship a-cross the

a-tion,___ held her hands out___ in the name of love there would
a-tion,___ held his hands out___ in the name of love there would
a-tion,___ hold ing hands out___ in the name of love there would
wa-ters,___ re - fus-ing___ to be en-e-mies there would

|1, 2, 3 | 4 |

be no more - war. 2. If ev'ry
be no more - war. 3. If ev'ry
be no more war. 4. If ev'ry war.
be no more

LAUS DEO (Redhead No. 46) 87.87.

R. Redhead, 1820-1901

74 In our childhood's understanding

In our childhood's understanding
life seemed limitless and free.
Now we face the contemplation
of our own mortality.

Life seemed simple spread before us,
now, distorted, futile, flawed;
child-like hope has been extinguished,
fear, with understanding, spawned.

Here in doubt and dereliction,
searching for the reason why,
hoping prayer might kindle kindness,
hoping you might hear our cry.

Now we're startled by the stillness,
stark surprise that you are there;
then we're blinded by the dazzle
of the dawning of your care!

Andrew Pratt b. 1948

DUDDON L.M.

David Dawson, b.1939

1.In quick-'ning streams and warm - ing earth,

in buds and root - lets grop - ing blind,

the world a - wakes and brings to birth e -

ter - nal hopes to hu - man - kind.

75 In quickening streams

In quickening streams and warming earth,
in buds and rootlets groping blind,
the world awakes and brings to birth
eternal hopes to humankind.

The aeons pass in cadence slow,
ideas through the centuries roam,
but all life forces blend and flow -
we harvest thoughts by others sown.

Each generation tries anew
and people venture to explore
old wisdom clad in raiment new,
fresh insight found in ancient lore.

A beacon from a far-off star
may touch a light-year distant soul.
A deed unmarked can travel far
and work to make a stranger whole.

Great good was wrought in ages past
when love and faith at wrongs were hurled:
so dare to change while life shall last,
take hold and shake a dormant world.

Janet H. Bowering

I SAW THREE SHIPS L.M.

Traditional Melody
Arr. Martin Shaw

76 In spring I saw the Easter tree

In spring I saw the Easter tree,
the Easter tree, the Easter tree;
in spring I saw the Easter tree,
the fairest gift in the garden.

'Twas tall and broad and fine to see,
and fine to see, and fine to see;
'twas tall and broad and fine to see,
the fairest tree in the garden.

The tree it was an evergreen,
an evergreen, an evergreen;
the tree it was an evergreen,
the fairest tree in the garden.

Its fruit did taste of pure delight,
of pure delight, of pure delight;
its fruit did taste of pure delight,
the fairest tree in the garden.

And of its fruit all may partake,
all may partake, all may partake;
and of its fruit all may partake,
the fairest tree in the garden.

Francis Simons 1939 - 1993

77 In the morning

THE MORNING SONG

Words and Music : Myrna Michell, b.1951

1.In the morn - ing, when the dawn___ leans far a-cross___ the land, take a mo - ment to re - call___ those lit - tle things___ you planned.

2.If the morn - ing's gloom - y,___ and all the world___ seems grey, don't turn o - ver in your bed;___ stand up and face___ the day.

Let your feel - ings fly,_____ they will not____ be
Make the dark clouds fly,_____ at your own____ com-

bound; stretch your voi - ces high;_____
mand; life is stand - ing by;_____

1.
send them all____ a - round.
take it by____ the

2.
hand.

Composer's note: The harmony repeats from the halfway point:-
so bars 1-8 can be sung with bars 9-16. Try different arrangements: e.g some
voices humming the melody or singing to 'la'; also try adding percussion instruments.

HEATON 8.8.8.   David Dawson, b.1939

Music © David Dawson 1985. Used by permission.

78 In the spring with plough and harrow

In the spring with plough and harrow,
farmers worked in field and furrow;
now we harvest for tomorrow.

Beauty adds to bounty's measure
giving freely for our pleasure
sights and sounds and scents to treasure.

But earth's garden will not flourish
if in greed we spoil and ravish
that which we should prize and cherish.

We must show a deeper caring,
show compassion to the dying,
cease from avarice and warring.

So may we at our thanksgiving
give this pledge to all things living:
that we will obey love's bidding.

John Andrew Storey 1935–1997

BEETHOVEN 87.87.D.

Adapted from Ludwig van Beethoven, 1770-1827

79 In this time on earth we're given

In this time on earth we're given
each to have a life to live.
May we make it nearer heaven
by our deeds and what we give.
May we see that acts of kindness,
gifts of love that never cease
help the world cast off its blindness,
bring to all the hope of peace.

By God's hand we were created
of the greater plan a part.
Long o'erdue the world has waited
for the human hand and heart.
Suffering we'll try to vanquish.
From our hearts all malice take.
Gladness, joy instead of anguish,
harmony, not discord, make.

A. Bronwen Taylor b. 1946

JUDAS AND MARY

Sydney Bertram Carter, 1915-2004

1.I - sai - ah the pro - phet has writ - ten of old how God's new cre - a - tion shall come.____ In-stead of the thorn tree, the fir tree shall grow and the wolf shall lie down with the lamb, the lamb, the wolf shall lie down with the lamb.____ joy.____

Music © 1964 Stainer & Bell Ltd, 23 Gruneisen Road, London N3 1DZ. www.stainer.co.uk

80 Isaiah the prophet has written

Isaiah the prophet has written of old
how God's new creation shall come.
Instead of the thorn tree, the fir tree shall grow
and the wolf shall lie down with the lamb, the lamb,
the wolf shall lie down with the lamb.

The mountains and hills shall break forth into song,
the peoples be led forth in peace;
the earth shall be filled with the knowledge of God
as the waters cover the sea, the sea,
as the waters cover the sea.

Yet nations still prey on the meek of the world,
and conflict turns parent from child.
Your people despoil all the sweetness of earth;
and the brier and the thorn tree grow wild, grow wild,
and the brier and the thorn tree grow wild.

God bring to fruition your will for the earth,
that no one shall hurt or destroy,
that wisdom and justice shall reign in the land
and your people shall go forth in joy, in joy,
your people shall go forth in joy.

Joy F. Patterson b. 1931

BUDAPEST 8.8.8.

Traditional Hungarian Melody: Régi egyházi ének
Arr. David Dawson

Music © 2009 Arrangement used by permission.

81 Isten, God of our confessing

Isten, God of our confessing,
Isten, light in deep distressing,
Isten, grant to us thy blessing.

Egy az Isten, one is holy,
one is God, our testimony,
one on earth and heaven only.

One, the blessed God we cherish,
body, spirit, wisdom nourish,
faith and freedom ever flourish.

Hungarian Unitarian ET by Jozsef Kaszoni

'Isten' = God; 'Egy az Isten' = 'God is one'; pronounced 'Edge Oz Eeshten'

Words ET © Jozsef Kaszoni.

LINDNER 10.10.11.10.

Carlton R. Young, b.1926

1.Joy - ful is the dark, ho - ly hid- den God, roll -ing cloud of night be-yond all nam - ing: maj - es-ty in dark - ness, en - er - gy of love, Word in flesh, the mys - ter- y pro - claim - ing. sto - ry!

vv 1-4

v.5

82 Joyful is the dark

1st verse is with the music

Joyful is the dark,
Spirit of the deep,
winging wildly o'er the world's creation,
silken sheen at midnight,
plumage black and bright,
swooping with the beauty of a raven.

Joyful is the dark,
shadowed stable floor;
angels flicker, God on earth confessing,
as with exultation,
Mary, giving birth,
hails the infant cry of need and blessing.

Joyful is the dark,
coolness in the tomb,
waiting for the wonder of the morning;
never was that midnight
touched by dread and gloom:
darkness was the cradle of the dawning.

Joyful is the dark,
depth of love divine,
roaring, looming thundercloud of glory,
holy, haunting beauty,
living, loving God.
Hallelujah! Sing and tell the story!

Brian Wren b. 1936

NICHT SO TRAURIG 77.77.77.

Johann G Ebeling, 1637-1676
Arr. David Dawson

83 Just as long as I have breath

Just as long as I have breath,
I must answer, "Yes," to life;
though with pain I made my way,
still with hope I meet each day.
If they ask what I did well,
tell them I said, "Yes," to life.

Just as long as vision lasts,
I must answer, "Yes," to truth;
in my dream and in my dark,
always that elusive spark.
If they ask what I did well,
tell them I said, "Yes," to truth.

Just as long as my heart beats,
I must answer, "Yes," to love;
disappointment pierced me through,
still I kept on loving you.
If they ask what I did best,
tell them I said, "Yes," to love.

Alicia S. Carpenter b. 1930

GEORGINA 11.10.11.10.

David Dawson, b.1939

1.Jus-tice for per - sons and for diff-'rent na - tions,
res-pect the di - verse spec - ies in our care,
com -mun-i - ty of life on earth sus -tain - ing,
love for this pla - net which we all must share.

84 Justice for persons

Justice for persons and for different nations,
respect the diverse species in our care,
community of life on earth sustaining,
love for this planet which we all must share.

Compassion is the strength of love and sympathy
letting us share another being's pain;
creature or human, loving friend or stranger,
love for each other is the whole world's gain.

Wisdom is insight clear, precise and thoughtful,
searching for truth and human law refined;
guidance from past, made ready for the future
by the best reasoning of the human mind.

Integrity, with honour and uprightness:
these are the qualities which form and make
women and men, the people for tomorrow,
those who serve others for another's sake.

Justice, compassion, wisdom and integrity,
these are the virtues which our poor world needs.
They'll flower tomorrow, fruit in glorious splendour,
if we today go out and plant the seeds.

Andrew McKean Hill b. 1942

LANGBAR 12.10.12.10. Dactylic

David Dawson, b.1939

1.Keep me from help - less - ness lead - ing to hope - less - ness;

Lord, be my guide through the dark - ness and strife.

Val - ue my be - ing, don't nur - ture my na - ked - ness;

lift me and love me, give mean - ing to life.

85 Keep me from helplessness

Keep me from helplessness leading to hopelessness;
Lord, be my guide through the darkness and strife.
Value my being, don't nurture my nakedness;
lift me and love me, give meaning to life.

Held in a prison house, crippled by prejudice,
share my captivity, silently care.
Face with me fearlessly folly's sheer edifice;
quietly and calmly, yes, simply be there.

Now, quite explosively, freedom and liberty
break on my being like infinite light;
dazzling my senses with love's creativity,
banishing darkness and ending the night!

Andrew Pratt, b. 1948

86 Lady of the seasons' laughter

JULION 87.87.87.

David Hurd, b.1950

1.La - dy
2.Sis - ter

of the sea - sons' laugh - ter, in the sum - mer's warmth be
of the eve - ning star - light, in the fall - ing sha - dows

near; when the win - ter fol - lows af - ter, teach our
stay here a - mong us till the far light of to -

spir - its not to fear. Hold us in your stea - dy
mor - row's dawn - ing ray. Hold us in your stea - dy

mer - cy, La - dy of the turn - ing year.
mer - cy, La - dy of the turn - ing day.

Last time

1st and 2nd verses with the music

Mother of the generations,
in whose love all life is worth
everlasting celebrations,
bring our labours safe to birth.
Hold us in your steady mercy,
Lady of the turning earth.

Goddess of all times' progression,
stand with us when we engage
hands and hearts to end oppression,
writing history's fairer page.
Hold us in your steady mercy,
Lady of the turning age.

Words: Kendyl Gibbons, b. 1955

CORINTH 87.87.87.

Melody from *Antiphons* (1792)
of Samuel Webbe, 1740-1816

87 Leave behind your bags and baggage

Leave behind your bags and baggage.
Throw all caution to the air.
Let the wind blow through the cobwebs.
Cast aside all anxious care.
Let the God of all our mercies
breathe around you everywhere.

Journey onwards never doubting
God will speak a kindly word,
looking forward, always trusting
what your heart feels will be heard.
Love your sister and your brother:
kindness will not be deterred.

In the face of war and hatred
peace and justice we extol.
Share the warmth of fellow-feeling
urging us onto our goal.
With your confidence enthuse us,
God, the life in every soul.

Peter Sampson b. 1938

Words © Peter Sampson. Used by permission.

88 Let it be a dance we do

MASTEN

Words and Music: Ric Masten, 1929-2008

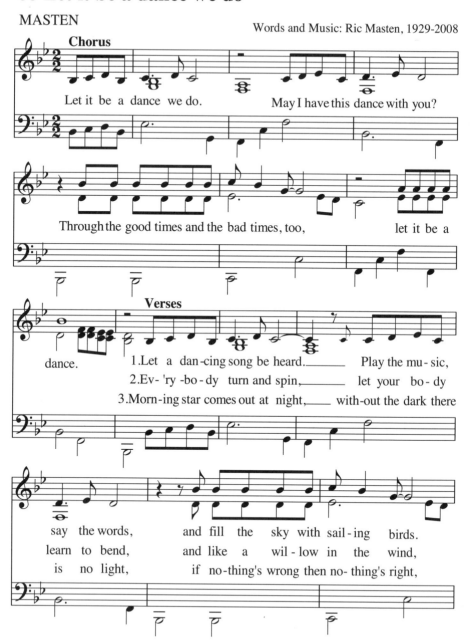

Let it be a dance. Let it be a dance. Let it be a
Let it be a dance. Let it be a dance. Let it be a
Let it be a dance. Let it be a dance. Let it be a

dance._____ Learn to fol - low, learn to lead,____
dance._____ A child is born, the old must die,____
dance._____ Let the sun shine, let it rain,____

____ feel the rhy - thm, fill the need_____ to reap the har - vest,
____ a time for joy, a time to cry,_____ take it as it
____ share the laugh-ter, bear the pain,_____ and round and round we

plant the seed,_____ Let it be a dance._____
pass - es by._____ Let it be a dance._____
go a - gain._____ Let it be a dance._____

CONCORD 4.7.7.6.

Robert J. B. Fleming, 1921-1976

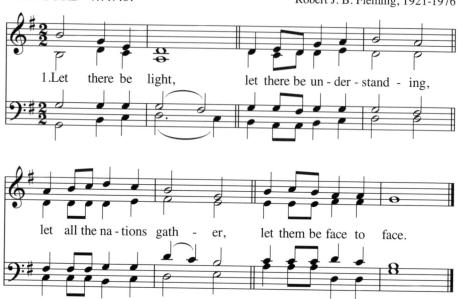

1.Let there be light, let there be un - der - stand - ing,
let all the na - tions gath - er, let them be face to face.

Music © Used by permission.

89 Let there be light

Let there be light,
let there be understanding,
let all the nations gather,
let them be face to face.

Open our lips,
open our minds to ponder,
open the doors of concord
opening into grace.

Perish the sword,
perish the angry judgment,
perish the bombs and hunger,
perish the fight for gain.

Let there be light,
open our hearts to wonder,
perish the way of terror,
hallow the world God made.

Frances W. Davis b. 1936

STOWEY 12.12.12.12.

English Traditional Melody
Arr. & Har. Ralph Vaughan Williams, 1872-1958

1.Let us give thanks and praise for the gifts which we share,

for our food and our friend - ship, for wa - ter and air,

for the earth and the sky and the stars and the sea,

and the trust we all have in God's love flow - ing free.

90 Let us give thanks and praise

Let us give thanks and praise for the gifts which we share,
for our food and our friendship, for water and air,
for the earth and the sky and the stars and the sea,
and the trust we all have in God's love flowing free.

Give a shout of amazement at what life can bring,
put your heart into raising the song all can sing.
What a world we could build with our minds and our hands
where the people live freely and God understands.

Let us give of our best with the tools we shall need,
use our eyes, hands and brains so that we may succeed.
Inspire us to cultivate what we have sown
so that nature and nurture make a world we may own.

We adore you, great Mother, O help us to live
with a love for each other that each one can give
let the pain of our brothers and sisters be faced
and the healing of all souls on earth be embraced.

Peter Sampson b. 1938

91 Let us give thanks

Joyce Poley, b.1941

Let us give thanks for the food that we share.
Let us give thanks for people who care.
Food fills the body and love makes us whole.
Let us give thanks deep down in our soul.

Words: Joyce Poley, b.1941

92 Let us renew our covenant

ST. BERNARD C.M.

Melody from Tochter Sion, 1741
Arr. John Richardson, 1816-1879

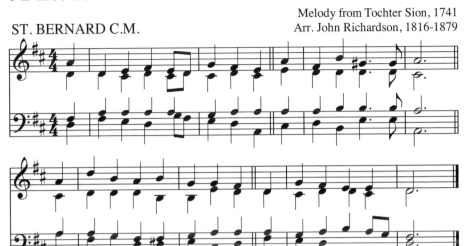

Let us renew our covenant
to build community,
within a place where justice reigns
and flowers, liberty;

a place for people of all kinds
and all abilities;
a place for people from all parts
and nationalities;

a place for people of all faiths
despite their difference,
their age, their colour or their race,
their sex or preference.

So bless, O God, our covenant
and bless this earthly place
which swings through stars and galaxies
and through the curves of space.

Words: Andrew McKean Hill b. 1942

HOLYWELL 87.87.D.

Harold William Spicer, 1888-1977

93 Let us sing of earth's progression

Let us sing of earth's progression
from the cruel, base and mean;
not all wrong and all transgression
has our story always been.
On good Francis birds alighted;
Kevin held his hand as nest;
human thought has wrought regression,
yet by humans, life is blest.

Such was Cuthbert's revelation;
he stood singing in the sea
as the seals in celebration
barked their *Benedicite.*
Though we take these tales as legend,
in them shines divinity
and we make our sung elation
for all insights gained of thee.

Not of force and domination
over land and air and sea,
but with love's co-operation
sing we this theology.
God of stars and God of spider,
God of fruitbat and of flower,
we are agents with creation
working with the Spirit's power.

Angus Martin Parker

The hymn refers to 3 Christian saints associated with animals:
1. St. Francis of Assisi 1181-1226
2. St. Kevin (5th century) Irish saint with an affinity for blackbirds
3. St. Cuthbert (d.687) who swam with the seals at Lindisfarne

GRACE SOIT RENDUE 65.65.D. + Refrain

French Canadian Carol Tune
Arr. David Dawson

1.Let us wel - come Chan - nu - kah, Jew-ish feast of light,
when quite un - ex - pec - ted and midst des - p'rate plight,
came to tired peo - ple with their spir-its low, plen - ti - ful re-
sour - ces of God's love to show: **Refrain** Al - le - lu - ia! Al - le - lu -
ia! Peace on earth, good - will ev' - ry - one, Al - le - lu - ia!

94 Let us welcome Channukah

1st verse is with the music

Let us welcome Yuletide
in this northern clime;
when in deep December
once again it's time
for us to make merry
and the long nights spurn,
bid the short days lengthen
and the sun return.
Alleluia! Alleluia!
Peace on earth, goodwill everyone, Alleluia!

Let us welcome Christmas
when an infant smiles
and from manger cradle
gently reconciles
all whose hearts are broken,
or who live with pain,
so that every person
may be whole again.
Alleluia! Alleluia!
Peace on earth, goodwill everyone, Alleluia!

At this festive season
let us all rejoice,
send the world a message
with a common voice.
Let our festive greeting
be that wars shall cease
and that all earth's people
learn to live in peace.
Alleluia! Alleluia!
Peace on earth, goodwill everyone, Alleluia!

Andrew McKean Hill b. 1942

WAS LEBET, WAS SCHWEBET 12.11.12.11.

From the *Rheinhardt MS,*
Uttingen, 1754

1. Let's praise the Cre - a - tor who gave us each oth - er
in friend - ship and kin - ship to cel - e - brate life;
let's sing our de - light in this man and this wom - an,
the prom - ise of joy as a hus - band and wife.

95 Let's praise the Creator

Let's praise the Creator who gave us each other
in friendship and kinship to celebrate life;
let's sing our delight in this man and this woman,
the promise of joy as a husband and wife.

The love that we wish them, the love that we pray for
is stronger than storms and more gentle than breath,
endures every trouble, is selfless and faithful,
more precious than life and more lasting than death.

In vows that are honoured, in kissing and blessing
may happiness shine like the gold of a ring;
in passionate joy and compassionate caring
may theirs be the gifts that true loving can bring.

Shirley Erena Murray b. 1931

LITTLE CORNARD 66.66.88. Dactylic

Martin Fallas Shaw, 1875-1958

96 Lord of our growing years

Lord of our growing years,
with us from infancy,
laughter and quick dried tears,
freshness and energy:
your grace surrounds us all our days;
for all your gifts we bring our praise.

Lord of our strongest years,
stretching our youthful powers,
lovers and pioneers
when all the world seems ours;
your grace surrounds us all our days;
for all your gifts we bring our praise.

Lord of our middle years,
giver of steadfastness,
courage that perseveres
when there is small success:
your grace surrounds us all our days;
for all your gifts we bring our praise.

Lord of our older years,
steep though the road may be,
rid us of foolish fears,
bring us serenity;
your grace surrounds us all our days;
for all your gifts we bring our praise.

Lord of our closing years,
always your promise stands;
hold us, when death appears,
safely within your hands.
your grace surrounds us all our days;
for all your gifts we bring our praise.

David Mowbray b. 1938

ANGEL'S CAMP C.M.

Daniel Charles Damon b.1955

97 Love knocks and waits for us to hear

Love knocks and waits for us to hear,
to open and invite;
love longs to quiet every fear,
and seeks to set things right.

Love offers life, in spite of foes
who threaten and condemn;
embracing enemies, love goes
the second mile with them.

Love comes to heal the broken heart,
to ease the troubled mind;
without a word love bids us start
to ask and seek and find.

Love knocks and enters at the sound
of welcome from within;
love sings and dances all around,
and feels new life begin.

Daniel Charles Damon b. 1955

OLYMPIA L.M.

Traditional Melody
Arr. David Dawson

1.Love___ will guide us, peace___ has tried___ us, hope in-
side___ us will lead the way_____ on the road___ from greed___ to
giv - ing. Love will guide___ us through the hard night.

Music © Arrangement used by permission.

98 Love will guide us

Love will guide us, peace has tried us,
hope inside us will lead the way
on the road from greed to giving.
Love will guide us through the hard night.

If you cannot sing like angels,
if you cannot speak before thousands,
you can give from deep within you.
You can change the world with your love.

Love will guide us, peace has tried us,
hope inside us will lead the way
on the road from greed to giving.
Love will guide us through the hard night.

Sally Rogers

ELLEN 87.87.

David Dell, b.1959

1. Lov-ing Spi - rit, lov- ing Spi - rit, you have cho - sen me to be; you have drawn me to your won - der, you have set your sign on me.

Verses 1-4
Verse 5
me.

99 Loving spirit, loving spirit

Loving spirit, loving spirit,
you have chosen me to be;
you have drawn me to your wonder,
you have set your sign on me.

Like a mother, you enfold me,
hold my life within your own,
feed me with your very body,
form me of your flesh and bone.

Like a father, you protect me,
teach me the discerning eye,
hoist me up upon your shoulder,
let me see the world from high.

Friend and lover, in your closeness
I am known and held and blessed:
in your promise is my comfort,
in your presence I may rest.

Loving spirit, loving spirit,
you have chosen me to be -
you have drawn me to your wonder,
you have set your sign on me.

Shirley Erena Murray b. 1931

FILLED WITH LOVING KINDNESS

Ian W. Riddell, b.1968

May I be filled_____ with lov-ing kind-ness.
May I be well._____ May I be filled_____ with lov-ing
kind-ness. May I be well._____ May I be
peace_____ful and at ease. May I be whole.

100 May I be filled with loving kindness

May I be filled with loving kindness.
May I be well.
May I be filled with loving kindness.
May I be well.
May I be peaceful and at ease.
May I be whole.

May you be filled with loving kindness.
May you be well.
May you be filled with loving kindness.
May you be well.
May you be peaceful and at ease.
May you be whole.

May we be filled with loving kindness.
May we be well.
May we be filled with loving kindness.
May we be well.
May we be peaceful and at ease.
May we be whole.

Buddhist meditation adapted by Mark W. Hayes b. 1949

101 May I use my hands with care

THEODORA   77.77.

George Frederick Handel, 1685-1759
From 'Theodora'

May I use my hands with care,
touching gently all I share.
May I with attentive ears
hear another's hopes and fears.

May I, using well my eyes,
notice what before me lies.
May I with my sense of smell
musk from mint distinguish well.

May I with my gift of taste
savour all things without haste.
All my senses I employ;
all Your gifts may I enjoy.

Words: Andrew McKean Hill b.1942

102 May the road rise with you

Traditional
Arr. David Dawson

A BLESSING

May the road rise with you, may the wind be al-ways at your back, may the sun shine warm up-on your face, may the rain fall soft up-on your fields, and un-til we meet a-gain, may God hold you in the hol-low of his/her hand.

MOTHER EARTH

Amanda Udis-Kessler, b.1965

1.Mo - ther Earth, be - lov - ed gar - den, liv - ing trea - sure un - der foot,

all our days you ground our be - ing: sage and this - tle, grass and root.

Herbs to heal us, plants to feed us, land to till and tend and plough

With the pen - dant, deep as mid -night, North we ask you: be here now._____

103 Mother Earth

Mother Earth, beloved garden, living treasure under foot,
all our days you ground our being: sage and thistle, grass and root.
Herbs to heal us, plants to feed us, land to till and tend and plough,
with the pendant, deep as midnight, North, we ask you: be here now.

Father Air, your inspiration holds together all that lives.
As we breathe, our minds see clearly, leading us to live and give.
Raging whirlwind, whispered breezes, violent gale and gentle cloud,
with the blade as sharp as morning, East, we ask you: be here now.

Brother Fire, great transformer, share the passion of the sun.
In our hearths, your warmth revives us, cooks our food and heats our homes.
Flaming candle, blood within us, blazing desert, will to grow.
With the wand, directing power, South, we ask you: be here now.

Sister Water, ever flowing, ocean, river, pond and rain,
drink we now and quench our thirsting; cleanse us, we begin again.
Mist and ice, a host of changes; all that courage will allow,
with the cup, the holy chalice, West, we ask you: be here now.

Lover Spirit, intuition in the centre of our souls.
In your love we find relation, all connected, we are whole.
Timeless mystery, quiet conscience, deepest values, voice inside,
with the drum and with the cauldron, this we ask you: be our guide.

Amanda Udis-Kessler b. 1965 (based on Francis of Assisi)

NAME UNNAMED

David Dawson, b.1939

Refrain

Name un - named, hid - den and shown, know-ing and known.

Glo____ ri - a._____ Fine Verses

1.Beau - ti-full-y mov - ing, cease - less - ly form - ing, grow - ing, e - merg - ing with awe - some de- light, Ma - ker of Rain - bows, glow - ing with col - our, arch - ing in won - der, en - er - gy flow - ing in dark - ness and light:

104 Name unnamed

Name unnamed, hidden and shown, knowing and known. Gloria!

Beautifully moving, ceaselessly forming,
growing, emerging with awesome delight,
Maker of Rainbows, glowing with colour, arching in wonder,
energy flowing in darkness and light:
Name unnamed, hidden and shown, knowing and known. Gloria

Spinner of Chaos, pulling and twisting,
freeing the fibres of pattern and form,
Weaver of Stories, famed or unspoken, tangled or broken,
shaping a tapestry vivid and warm:
Name unnamed, hidden and shown, knowing and known. Gloria

Nudging Discomforter, prodding and shaking,
waking our lives to creative unease,
Straight-Talking Lover, checking and humbling, jargon and grumbling,
speaking the truth that refreshes and frees:
Name unnamed, hidden and shown, knowing and known. Gloria

Midwife of Changes, skilfully guiding,
drawing us out through the shock of the new,
Woman of Wisdom, deeply perceiving, never deceiving,
freeing and leading in all that we do:
Name unnamed, hidden and shown, knowing and known. Gloria

Daredevil Gambler, risking and loving,
giving us freedom to shatter your dreams,
Life-giving Loser, wounded and weeping, dancing and leaping,
sharing the caring that heals and redeems.
Name unnamed, hidden and shown, knowing and known. Gloria

Brian Wren, born 1936

EASTER HYMN 77.77.+ Alleluias

Melody in Lyra Davidica, 1708

105 Nature shouts from earth and sky

Nature shouts from earth and sky, Alleluia!
In the spring our spirits fly, Alleluia!
Join the resurrection cry, Alleluia!
Love is God and fears must die, Alleluia!

Mary's son, Christ Jesus, died, Alleluia!
Killed by humans full of pride, Alleluia!
Such a loss of such a friend, Alleluia!
Yet the cross was not the end, Alleluia!

Out of death his spirit sings, Alleluia!
Love to all the earth he brings, Alleluia!
Telling nations, war must cease, Alleluia!
Sisters, brothers, join in peace, Alleluia!

Christian, Muslim, Buddhist, Jew, Alleluia!
All are ways for love in you, Alleluia!
Many rainbows share one sun, Alleluia!
In the many, God is one, Alleluia!

Richard Boeke b. 1931

MANY MANSIONS 55.54.D.

Peter Cutts, b.1937

1.No - thing dis- tress you, no - thing af -fright you, ev- 'ry-thing

pass - es, God will a - bide. Pa - tient en- dea -vour ac-com-plish-es

all things; who God pos -sess - es needs naught be -side.

106 Nothing distress you

Nothing distress you,
nothing affright you,
everything passes,
God will abide.
Patient endeavour
accomplishes all things;
who God possesses
needs naught beside.

Lift your mind upward,
fair are his mansions,
nothing distress you,
cast fear away.
Follow Christ freely,
his love will light you,
nothing affright you,
in the dark way.

See the world's glory!
Fading its splendour,
everything passes,
all is denied.
Look ever homeward
to the eternal;
faithful in promise
God will abide.

Love in due measure,
measureless goodness,
patient endeavour,
run to love's call!
Faith burning brightly
be your soul's shelter;
who hopes, believing,
accomplishes all.

Hell may assail you,
it cannot move you;
sorrows may grieve you,
faith may be tried.
Though you have nothing,
he is your treasure:
who God possesses
needs naught beside.

St. Teresa of Avila 1515-1582 translated Colin Peter Thompson b. 1945

107 Now let us sing

ROBESON

Anonymous

Note: The small notes in the 'alto' provide an optional third part
and a fuller accompaniment.

108 Now rejoice!

Robert Waller

JOEL(2) 88.88.88.

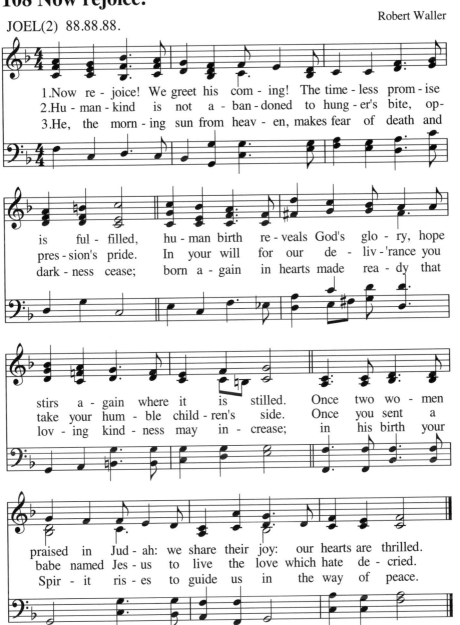

1.Now re - joice! We greet his com - ing! The time - less prom - ise
2.Hu - man - kind is not a - ban - doned to hung - er's bite, op-
3.He, the morn - ing sun from heav - en, makes fear of death and

is ful - filled, hu - man birth re - veals God's glo - ry, hope
pres - sion's pride. In your will for our de - liv - 'rance you
dark - ness cease; born a - gain in hearts made rea - dy that

stirs a - gain where it is stilled. Once two wo - men
take your hum - ble child - ren's side. Once you sent a
lov - ing kind - ness may in - crease; in his birth your

praised in Jud - ah: we share their joy: our hearts are thrilled.
babe named Jes - us to live the love which hate de - cried.
Spir - it ris - es to guide us in the way of peace.

Words: Clifford Martin Reed, b.1947

NOEL NOUVELET 11.10.10.11.

Medieval French carol,
Arr. Marcel Dupré, 1886-1971

1.Now the green blade ri - seth from the___ bur - ied grain,

wheat___ that in dark earth ma - ny___ days has lain;

love lives a - gain, that with the dead has been:___

Love is come a - gain, like wheat that___ spring - eth green.

109 Now the green blade riseth

Now the green blade riseth from the buried grain,
wheat that in dark earth many days has lain;
Love lives again, that with the dead has been:
>   *Love is come again,*
>   *like wheat that springeth green.*

In the grave they laid him, Love by hatred slain,
thinking that never he would wake again,
laid in the earth like grain that sleeps unseen:
>   *Love is come again,*
>   *like wheat that springeth green.*

Forth he came at Easter, like the risen grain,
he that for three days in the grave had lain,
quick from the dead my risen Lord is seen:
>   *Love is come again,*
>   *like wheat that springeth green.*

When our hearts are wintry, grieving, or in pain,
Love's touch can call us back to life again,
fields of our hearts that dead and bare have been:
>   *Love is come again,*
>   *like wheat that springeth green.*

John MacLeod Campbell Crum 1872-1958

OLICANA 84.84.888.4

Music: David Dawson, b.1939

1.Now we sing to praise love's bless-ing all through our lives, laugh-ter, joy, sur-prise, con-fess-ing all through our lives, love that dreamed a new cre-a-tion, love that dares through in-car-na-tion, love that off-ers trans-for-ma-tion all through our lives.

110 Now we sing to praise love's blessing

1st verse is with the music

How our wounds ache for love's healing
   all through our days;
how our world needs love's revealing
   in all its ways.
Fearful hearts suspect the stranger,
hardened nations arm for danger,
love live on, the powerful changer,
   all through our days.

Love's the grace that makes us caring
   all through our lives,
urges us to warmth and sharing
   all through our lives,
speaks in us, oppression naming,
strives in us. injustice shaming,
lives in us, true peace proclaiming
   all through our lives.

Love's the clown that mocks at winning
   all through the world,
midwife of each new beginning
   all through the world,
in the struggles that confound us,
in the chaos all around us
love's wide arms with hope surround us
   all through the world.

In God's faithful love we flourish
   all through our lives,
known and loved, each other nourish
   all through our lives;
though the world's demands are pressing,
what life brings is left to guessing,
still we sing to praise love's blessing
   all through our lives.

Anna Briggs Words © Anna Briggs

111 O Brother Sun

Traditonal Scottish Melody
Arr. David Dawson

YE BANKS AND BRAES L.M.D.

1. O Bro - ther Sun,— you bring— us light,— all
2. O Bro - ther Fire,— you warm— our night— with

shin - ing 'round— in fi - 'ry might. O—
all— your danc - ing col - oured light. O—

Sis - ter Moon,— you heal— and bless,— your
Sis - ter Earth,— you feed— all things,— all

beau— ty shines— in ten - der - ness. O
birds,— all crea - tures, all scales and wings. O

Bro - ther Wind,___ you sweep the hills,___ your
Sis - ter Death,___ you meet us here___ and

migh - ty breath___ both fre - shens and fills. O___
take___ us to___ our God___ so___ near. O___

Sis - ter Wa - ter, you cleanse___ and flow___ through
God of Life,___ we give___ you praise___ for

ri - vers and streams,___ in ice___ and snow.
all___ your crea - tures, for all___ your ways.

Words: Sharon Anway, b.1951 (adapted from St. Francis of Assisi)

SAN ROCCO C.M.

Derek Williams, 1945-2007

1.O____ God, our words can-not ex - press____ the pain we feel this day.____ En - raged, un - cer - tain, we con - fess our need to bow and pray.

112 O God, our words cannot express

O God, our words cannot express
the pain we feel this day.
Enraged, uncertain, we confess
our need to bow and pray.

We grieve for all who lost their lives
and for each injured one.
We pray for children, husbands, wives
whose grief has just begun.

O Lord, we're called to offer prayer
for all our leaders, too.
May they, amid such great despair,
be wise in all they do.

We trust your mercy and your grace;
in you we will not fear!
May peace and justice now embrace!
Be with your people here!

Carolyn Winfrey Gillette

AMAZING GRACE C.M.

Traditional Melody
Arr. David Dawson

113 O God, the source of love and joy

O God, the source of love and joy
and strength to face each day,
take these thy children in thine hand,
and guide them on their way.

Our Father, giver of true love
on earth and from above,
bless now the promise that is made,
and seal it with thy love.

Thy love encircles all our lives,
and lets not go its hold;
O, may that bond of love unite
these two like rings of gold.

Now blessed be their pilgrimage –
and honesty their friend;
be with them, God of love and joy,
until the very end.

D. Elwyn Davies 1927-1997

LERWICK C.M.

David Dawson, b.1939

1.O God who made___ this earth un-spoiled___ a place for
us to dwell;___ you gave us life and pow'r to
choose___ to make it heav'n or hell.___

Music © David Dawson 2009. Used by permission.

114 O God who made this earth unspoiled

O God who made this earth unspoiled
a place for us to dwell;
you gave us life and power to choose
to make it heaven or hell.

In living we must do our best
to find the good, the true;
with joyous hearts, enquiring minds
to look at life anew.

Abundant life that's rich in love
brings blessings here on earth;
it seeks out strengths and qualities
and sees in each their worth.

O God, we ask that our life's search
springs from a love of you;
that through our thoughts, our acts and words
we will our faith renew.

A. Bronwen Taylor b. 1946

ST. CECILIA 66.66.

Leighton George Hayne, 1836-83

115 O God, O Spirit free

O God, O Spirit free,
source of unfolding life,
through you all comes to be,
creative mystery.

You have revealed your will
where we create and care,
where folk are striving still
with love their lives to fill.

Your gift - a vision bright
of people loving, new,
and we, in darksome night,
find courage at the sight.

Your kingdom, like a star,
illuminates the soul,
and building it we are,
though glimpsing it afar.

This earth - my labour's field,
its loving care my task,
help me my heart to yield
now that my way's revealed.

O Thou, O God within,
who gave your prophets strength,
come pour your spirit in,
make me their worthy kin.

Clifford Martin Reed b. 1947

Melody in *As Hymnodus Sacer*, Leipzig (1625)
Harmony: Felix Mendelssohn, 1809-1847

1.O let us now our voi - ces raise in in - vo - ca - tion__ and in praise; O let us sing with hearts in - spired by love that's ev - er mind - ful fired.

116 O let us now our voices raise

O let us now our voices raise
in invocation and in praise;
O let us sing with hearts inspired
by love that's ever mindful fired.

For though we sing a mighty song,
louder than any angel throng,
the veil of truth will not be rent
unless each word is thought and meant.

For though we sing as angels sweet
our melodies will not be meet,
no holy purpose will they find
unless our hearts be warm and kind.

So, sing we loud and sing we well,
word, thought and heart our loving tell!
Let our compassion fill the air,
our hymn a true and worthy prayer!

Peter Galbraith b. 1928

David Dawson, b.1939

Music © David Dawson 2009. Used by permission.

117 O Lord now give us strength

O Lord, now give us strength,
and in that strength divine,
we ask for knowledge, too,
the knowledge that is thine;

and in that knowledge, Lord,
grant to us in our days
an understanding heart
to see each other's ways;

and when we understand -
to understand the right,
the right which we may love,
and love with all our might,

the Essence we may love
upon which life has stood,
the essence which is God,
my God, and all that's good.

D. Elwyn Davies 1927-1997 based on Iolo Morganwg 1747-1827

Dyro, Dduw, dy naw erth, deall;
Ac yn neall, gwybod;
Ac yng ngwybod, gwybod y cyfiawn;
Ac yng ngwybod y cyfiawn, eigarn;
Ac a garu, caru pob hanfod;
Ac ym mhob hanfod, caru Duw,
Duw a phob daioni. [*Iolo Morganwg's Gorsedd Pareyer*]

[*ET*] Grant, O God, your protection; and in protection, strength; and in strength, understanding; and in understanding, perception; and in perception, perception of righteousness; and in perception of righteousness, the love of it; and in the love of it the love of all Life; and in all Life to love God, God and all goodness.

Hans Leo Hassler, 1564-1612
Har. Johann Sebastian Bach, 1685-1750

118 O sacred earth, now wounded

O sacred earth, now wounded,
what have we done to thee?
The carnage is unbounded,
for all our eyes to see.
Thy air and soil and water
are poisoned by our greed;
thy forests we do slaughter
to serve our every need.

So fierce in our ambitions
we've entered sunlight's field,
and armed with strong emissions
we've torn apart its shield;
and ever there is waiting
our bomb's immortal fire,
the flower of all our hating,
eternal glowing pyre.

The time has come for grieving,
to bow our heads, and pause;
and we must cease believing
that we may break earth's laws.
The time has come to worship
this place, where we belong;
to consecrate our earthship
with prayer, and verse, and song.

And then to start restoring
our earth, with our own hands,
with work, with love outpouring,
with laws throughout the lands;
to bring the nations nearer
with every quest for peace,
until, as hope grows clearer,
our war on earth may cease.

Martha M. Pikrell

KING'S LYNN 76. 76.D.

English Traditional Melody
Arr. Ralph Vaughan Williams, 1872-1958

1.O Source of ma - ny cul - tures, of__ lives, be-liefs and faith;

you brought us all to - ge - ther to share one world in space.

Now show us how to__ hon - our each vi - sion of your way,

to live with- in the ten - sion of diff -'rence you dis - play.

119 O Source of many cultures

O Source of many cultures,
of lives, beliefs and faith;
you brought us all together
to share one world in space.
       Now show us how to honour
       each vision of your way,
       to live within the tension
       of difference you display.

The colour and the culture,
that kept us both apart,
are gifts that we can offer,
a means for us to start
       a journey with each other
       till hand in hand we show,
       through mutual understanding,
       respect and love can grow.

Andrew Pratt b. 1948

120 O we give thanks

Wendy Luella Perkins
Arr. Charlie Walker

O, we give thanks_____ for this pre - cious day,_____
for all gath - er'd here_____ and those far a - way;_____
for this time we share_____ with love and care,_____
(food)*
O, we give thanks_____ for this pre - cious

*For use when sung as a mealtime grace

Additional words for solstice celebrations:

Winter Solstice:

O we give thanks for this shortest day,
for the solstice tree, children at play,
for birds that sing, the promise of spring,
O we give thanks for this shortest day.

Summer Solstice:

O we give thanks for this longest day,
for the gentle breeze, children at play.
Good-bye to spring, to summer we sing,
O we give thanks for this longest day.

COOLINGE 10.10.10.10.

Cyril Vincent Taylor, 1907-1991

1.O yearn - ing hearts, who long for peace to reign,

whose age - long prayers have echo - ed all in vain,

who weep and mourn for mill - ions dead and gone –

still is our cry, 'How long, dear___ God, how long?'

121 O yearning hearts

O yearning hearts, who long for peace to reign,
whose age-long prayers have echoed all in vain,
who weep and mourn for millions dead and gone -
still is our cry, 'How long, dear God, how long?'

Through sad long years the battle-cry of strife
has cut a swathe of grief in human life:
in our own time the weaponry of war
has claimed more lives than ever known before.

Still tyrants rule and persecute for power,
and in this world, e'en in this very hour,
people still languish, lost in lonely cell,
tortured and maimed in some unheeded hell.

Still lust and greed build war-machines of steel;
famine is used to bring the weak to heel,
and starving children plead with hungry eye -
can we ignore the eternal human cry?

From far-off cries we are no more immure;
slaughter and war can we no more endure;
one world are we, one family, one kin -
come, humankind, your new age usher in.

Hope, surging up from every human heart,
one song of peace from nations far apart -
now faintly heard, yet ever growing strong,
the chorus of a new millennium song.

Sydney Henry Knight 1923-2004

MEIRIONYDD 76.76.D.

William Lloyd, 1786-1852

122 O young and fearless Prophet

O young and fearless Prophet
of ancient Galilee,
your life is still a summons
to serve humanity,
to make our thoughts and actions
less prone to please the crowd,
to stand with humble courage
for truth with hearts unbowed.

O help us stand unswerving
against war's bloody way,
where hate and lust and falsehood
hold back your holy sway;
forbid false love of country,
that turns us from your call
who lifts above the nation
the neighbourhood of all.

Create in us the splendour
that dawns when hearts are kind,
that knows not race nor station
as boundaries of the mind;
that learns to value beauty,
in heart, or mind, or soul,
and longs to see God's children
as sacred, perfect, whole.

Stir up in us a protest
against unneeded wealth,
for some go starved and hungry
who plead for work and health.
Once more give us your challenge
above our noisy day,
and come to lead us forward
along your holy way.

S. Ralph Harlow, altered, 1885-1972

123 On the dusty earth drum

CAMBER 65.65.

Martin Shaw, 1875-1958

On the dusty earth drum
beats the falling rain;
now a whispered murmur,
now a louder strain.

Slender silvery drumsticks
on an ancient drum
beat the mellow music
bidding life to come.

Chords of life awakened,
notes of greening spring,
rise and fall triumphant
over everything.

Slender, silvery drumsticks
beat the long tattoo-
God, the Great Musician,
calling life anew.

Words: Joseph S. Cotter Jr. 1895-1919

124 One more step

Joyce Poley, b.1941

One more step, we will take one more step,
'til there is peace for us and everyone, we'll take one more step.

One more word, we will say one more word,
'til every word is heard by everyone, we'll say one more word.

One more prayer, we will say one more prayer,
'til every prayer is shared by everyone, we'll say one more prayer.

One more song, we will sing one more song,
'til every song is sung by everyone, we'll sing one more song.

Words: Joyce Poley, b.1941

SOUTHCOTE 99.79.+ Refrain

Sydney Bertram Carter, 1915-2004
Arr. David Dawson

1.One more step a-long the world I go, one more step a-long the world I go; from the old things to the new, keep me tra-vel-ling a-long with you; and it's from the old I tra-vel to the new, keep me tra-vel-ling a-long with you.

125 One more step along the world I go

One more step along the world I go,
one more step along the world I go;
from the old things to the new,
keep me travelling along with you;
and it's from the old I travel to the new,
keep me travelling along with you.

Round the corners of the world I turn,
more and more about the world I learn;
all the new things that I see
you'll be looking at along with me;
and it's from the old I travel to the new,
keep me travelling along with you.

As I travel through the bad and good,
keep me travelling the way I should;
where I see no way to go
you'll be telling me the way, I know;
and it's from the old I travel to the new,
keep me travelling along with you.

Give me courage when the world is rough,
keep me loving though the world is tough;
leap and sing in all I do,
keep me travelling along with you;
and it's from the old I travel to the new,
keep me travelling along with you.

You are older than the world can be,
you are younger than the life in me;
ever old and ever new,
keep me travelling along with you;
and it's from the old I travel to the new,
keep me travelling along with you.

Sydney Carter 1915-2004

OPEN THE DOOR

Joyce Poley, b.1941

1.O - pen the door, step right in - side, come in - to this place where love and hope will a - bide. Reach out your hand, I'll wel - come you in, it's so good to be to - ge - ther a - gain.

126 Open the door, step right inside

Open the door, step right inside,
come into this place where love and hope will abide.
Reach out your hand, I'll welcome you in,
it's so good to be together again.

Start out the day wearing a grin,
joyful faces make people want to come in.
Open your arms to show that you care,
and our little light will shine everywhere.

When you're in pain, trouble or doubt,
let the love come in to help the hurting get out.
Open your heart to share how you feel,
and we'll build a church of love that is real.

Open the door, step right inside,
come into this place where love and hope will abide.
Reach out your hand, I'll welcome you in,
it's so good to be together again.

Joyce Poley b. 1941

127 Open the window children

Elise Witt, b.1953

O-pen the win-dow chil-dren, o-pen the win-dow now.____

O-pen the win-dow chil-dren, o-pen the win-dow let the

dove fly in. O-pen the win-dow let the dove fly in.

1.Ma -
2.Neigh-
3.Bor -
4.Some
5.This

- ma and____ Pa - pa are fight - ing like____ snakes.
- bours lock their doors,___ build fen - ces so____ high.
- ders round___ coun - tries, bor - ders 'round the sky.
peo - ple have___ mon - ey, some peo - ple have___ none.
big old world is in___ a___ great___ big___ mess.

CHERNOBYL 5.8 8.6 4.

Cecily Taylor, b.1930
Arr. Richard Graves, 1926-2002

Unison

1.Our world is___ one world: what tou - ches
one af-fects us all — the seas that wash us round a- bout, the
clouds that co - ver us,_____ the rains that fall.

Music © 1988 Stainer & Bell Ltd, 23 Gruneisen Road, London N3 1DZ. www.stainer.co.uk

254

128 Our World is one world

Our world is one world:
what touches one affects us all —
the seas that wash us round about,
the clouds that cover us,
the rains that fall.

Our world is one world:
the thoughts we think affect us all —
the way we build our attitudes,
with love or hate, we make
a bridge or wall.

Our world is one world:
its ways of wealth affect us all —
the way we spend, the way we share,
who are the rich or poor,
who stand or fall?

Our world is one world,
just like a ship that bears us all —
where fear and greed make many holes,
but where our hearts can hear
a different call.

Cecily Taylor b. 1930

READING 88.88.88.

Francis Westbrook, 1903-1975

1.Ours is a gift, re- ceived from source of life at -tend-ing plan - ets' birth; and through the ae-ons it has striv'n un- til it flower'd in life on earth. *Giv - er of gifts, thanks for the grace which holds our lives in love's em - brace.*

129 Ours is a gift

Ours is a gift, received from source
of life attending planets' birth;
and through the aeons it has striven
until it flowered in life on earth.
> *Giver of gifts, thanks for the grace*
> *which holds our lives in love's embrace.*

Ours is a gift, whose source is found
in fundamental particles;
and after many vain attempts
came forth in living miracles.
> *Giver of gifts, thanks for the grace*
> *which holds our lives in love's embrace.*

Ours is a gift, whose messages
are passed along by coded seeds,
and issues forth with rich array
in countless million lives and deeds.
> *Giver of gifts, thanks for the grace*
> *which holds our lives in love's embrace.*

* for general use
Life is a gift; the grace of joy
and hope is by each person known;
and when in others we see the gift
we know grace has to them been shown.
> *Giver of gifts, thanks for the grace*
> *which holds our lives in love's embrace.*

* when celebrating a birth
This child's a gift! The grace of joy
and hope is by these parents known;
and round the world the message runs
'new possibilities are shown'.
> *Giver of gifts, thanks for the grace*
> *which holds our lives in love's embrace.*

Andrew McKean Hill b. 1942

RODMELL C.M.

English Traditional Melody
Coll. and Arr. Ralph Vaughan Williams, 1872-1958

130 Ours is a town for everyone

Ours is a town for everyone
who wants to play their part
in making it a better place
to practise living's art.

Ours is a town where every faith,
all creeds of hope and peace,
can worship freely, yet recall
we are one human race.

Ours is a town where we must care
for those whose lives are hard,
for whom bright mornings turn to tears
and all once fair seems marred.

Ours is a town where, side by side
in friendship and goodwill,
we'll build a place where all can be
respected and fulfilled.

So let us celebrate our town
and pledge ourselves to be
the ones who make it beautiful,
safe, prosperous and free.

Clifford Martin Reed b. 1947

131 Out of the depths I call to you

GRÄFENBURG (Nun Danket All) C.M.   Praxis Pietatis Melica, 1653

1.Out of the depths I call to you;— God give me power to - day.

In this dark time let me be true,— till storms have blown a - way.

1st verse with the music

From everything and everyone,
from all life left alone;
alone, despairing, faith undone,
my heart has turned to stone.

Beside me only you remain,
my comforter and friend;
your faithfulness my heart sustains,
"I know this night will end!"

The struggle of my life and pain
fade in the cosmic scheme:
a glimmer in a drop of rain,
lost in the battle's dream.

Again, I come to pray in haste,
O God, thanks be to thee;
may all who suffer find your grace,
and may I faithful be.

Words: Norbert Capek, 1879-1942.
ET Bodhana Hasplova and Richard Boeke, b.1931

132 Perfect Singer, songs of earth

ORIENTIS PARTIBUS 77.77.   From the Beauvais Liturgical Play, 13th Century

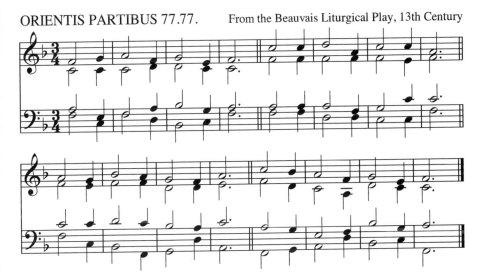

Perfect Singer, songs of earth
rise on every field and hearth;
let our voices sound again
ancient songs of joy and pain.

All your creatures strive for life,
suffer hurt and angry strife,
seek compassion, find release
in the covenant of peace.

Sing a sacred melody
for the justice that shall be;
let our harmonies resolve
dissonance in steadfast love.

Steadfast Seeker, find our song
woven into lives made strong;
let the patterns of surprise
kindle hope with each sunrise.

George Kimmich Beach, b.1935

RYBURN 88.88.88.

Norman Cocker, 1889-1953

1.Play trum-pet, 'cel - lo, harp and flute; play org-an, vi - o -
lin and lute. Write poems and read the writ - ten word;
write plays, tell stor - ies to be heard; and let the cos - mos
all___ a-round with love and jus - tice then re-sound.

133 Play trumpet, 'cello, harp and flute

Play trumpet, 'cello, harp and flute;
play organ, violin and lute.
Write poems and read the written word;
write plays, tell stories to be heard;
and let the cosmos all around
with love and justice then resound.

Paint pictures dark and paintings bright;
paint with a brush and paint with light.
Dance minuet and highland fling;
dance two by two and in a ring;
and let the cosmos all around
with love and justice then resound.

Speak words of comfort and of peace;
speak gently so that wars may cease.
Sing melodies and measured phrase;
sing songs to set the world ablaze;
and let the cosmos all around
with love and justice then resound.

Andrew McKean Hill b. 1942

OLD 124TH 10.10.10.10.10.

Genevan Psalter, 1551

134 Praise God for Michael

Praise God for Michael, honoured child of Spain,
land of the sunshine, also land of pain.
Jews, Moors and Christians trying to be one
but three-fold dogma means it can't be done.
Praise God for Michael, honoured child of Spain.

Praise God for Michael, true renaissance man
who first describes the holy spirit's plan
as like a body circulates its blood:
so light from Christ disperses in a flood.
Praise God for Michael, true renaissance man.

Praise God for Michael, scholar of the page,
student of languages from every age,
who reads his Bible searching for the three
but what he finds is damned with heresy.
Praise God for Michael, scholar of the page.

Praise God for Michael, brazen, wild and bold;
enters Geneva and the tyrant's fold
where he is captured and condemned to burn:
making a lesson for the world to learn.
Praise God for Michael, brazen, wild and bold.

"Sweet Jesus, pity: God Eternal's son."
People still struggle, freedom's scarcely won.
May we who honour Michael and his kind
still work to free the body and the mind.
"Sweet Jesus, pity: God Eternal's son."

Andrew McKean Hill b. 1942

Servetus' alleged last words, 27th October 1553, were "Jesus, son of the Eternal God, have mercy on me". Had he said "Jesus, Eternal Son of God" he would have been saved from the fire.

STOWEY 11.11.11.11

English Traditional Melody
Arr. & Harm. Ralph Vaughan Williams, 1872-1958

135 Praise God for the harvest

Praise God for the harvest of orchard and field,
praise God for the people who gather their yield,
the long hours of labour, the skills of a team,
the patience of science, the power of machine.

Praise God for the harvest that comes from afar,
from market and harbour, the sea and the shore:
foods packed and transported, and gathered and grown
by God-given neighbours, unseen and unknown.

Praise God for the harvest that's quarried and mined,
then sifted, and smelted, or shaped and refined;
for oil and for iron, for copper and coal,
praise God, who in love has provided them all.

Praise God for the harvest of science and skill,
the urge to discover, create and fulfil:
for dreams and inventions that promise to gain
a future more hopeful, a world more humane.

Praise God for the harvest of mercy and love
for leaders and peoples who struggle and serve
with patience and kindness, that all may be led
to freedom and justice, and all may be fed.

Brian Wren b. 1936

BOSCOMBE 87.87.D.

Michael Dawney

1.Praise the source of faith and learn - ing that has sparked and
stoked the mind with a pas - sion for dis - cern - ing
how the world has been de - signed. Let the sense of
won - der flow-ing from the won-ders we sur - vey keep our faith for-
ev - er grow - ing and re - new our need to pray.

136 Praise the source

1st verse with the music

Source of wisdom, we acknowledge
that our science and our art
and the breadth of human knowledge
only partial truth impart.
Far beyond our calculation
lies a depth we cannot sound
where the purpose for creation
and the pulse of life are found.

May our faith redeem the blunder
of believing that our thought
has displaced the grounds for wonder
which the ancient prophets taught.
May our learning curb the error
which unthinking faith can breed
lest we justify some terror
with an antiquated creed.

Praise for minds to probe the heavens,
praise for strength to breathe the air,
praise for all that beauty leavens,
praise for silence, music, prayer,
praise for justice and compassion
and for strangers, neighbours, friends,
praise for hearts and lips to fashion
praise for love that never ends.

Thomas H. Troeger b. 1945

CORVEDALE 87.87.D.

Maurice Bevan, 1921-2006

137 Praise to God, the world's Creator

Praise to God, the world's Creator,
source of life and growth and breath,
cradling in her arms her children,
holding them from birth to death.
In our bodies, in our living,
strength and truth of all we do,
God is present, working with us,
making us creators too.

Praise to God, our saving Wisdom,
meeting us with love and grace,
helping us to grow in wholeness,
giving freedom, room and space.
In our hurting, in our risking,
in the thoughts we dare not name,
God is present, growing with us,
healing us from pride and shame.

Praise to God, the Spirit in us,
prompting hidden depths of prayer,
firing us to long for justice,
reaching out with tender care.
In our searching, in our loving,
in our struggles to be free,
God is present, living in us,
pointing us to what shall be.

Jan Berry b. 1953

MARCHING 87.87.

Martin Fallas Shaw, 1875-1958

138 Red the poppy-fields of Flanders

Red the poppy-fields of Flanders,
red the Western Desert sands,
red the snows of Mother Russia:
red with blood that stains our hands.

We remember those who died there;
we must not forget their pain.
We remember all earth's children
whom the gods of war have slain.

Some have died for truth and justice,
died so others might be free.
Some have died for cause ignoble,
died the tools of tyranny.

Red the mud-drowned filth of trenches,
red the ruins once so fair,
red the jungles, red the oceans,
red the one blood that we share.

We would heed the pleading voices
of the folk who died for peace;
grant us now your loving Spirit,
that in us all strife may cease.

Clifford Martin Reed b. 1947

TENDERNESS 5.5.10.D.

Colin Alexander Gibson, b.1933

1. Sa - cred the bo - dy God has cre - a - ted, tem - ple of spi - rit that dwells deep in - side.___ Cher - ish each per - son, nur - ture re - la - tion, treat flesh as ho - ly that love may a - bide.___

Note: This tune is printed a semitone lower, in A major, at No.179

139 Sacred the body

Sacred the body
God has created,
temple of spirit that dwells deep inside.
Cherish each person,
nurture relation,
treat flesh as holy that love may abide.

Bodies are varied,
made in all sizes,
pale, full of colour, both fragile and strong.
Holy the difference,
gift of the Maker,
so let us honour each story and song.

Love respects persons,
bodies and boundaries;
love does not batter, neglect or abuse.
Love touches gently,
never coercing;
love leaves the other with power to choose.

Holy of holies,
God ever loving,
make us your temples; indwell all we do.
May we be careful,
tender and caring,
so may our bodies give honour to you.

Ruth C. Duck b. 1947

FELLOWSHIP 8.8.7.

Frank R. Clabburn, 1947-2000

1.See the mother's des - o - la - tion underneath the cross de - jec - ted where the child of her womb hangs.

140 See the mother's desolation

See the mother's desolation
underneath the cross dejected
where the child of her womb hangs.

Centuries of sacrificing
on the altar of our own cause
have not slaked the thirst for blood.

So this hatred still destroys us,
numbs our minds and kills compassion,
sure of only what we fear.

Help, O help us, God of healing,
help us in our self-willed blindness;
come to aid us trapped in pride.

Hold us, keep us, warm us, cure us,
lead us to embrace our kindred
in one worldwide loving home.

Peter Sampson b. 1938

141 She comes with mother's kindnesses

ST. BOTOLPH C.M.

Gordon Slater, 1896-1979

1.She comes with mo-ther's kind ness-es and bends to touch and heal. She gives her heart a-way in love for those who can-not feel.

1st verse with the music

She comes with lover's tenderness
to answer love's appeal.
She gives her body with her heart
to make her passion real.

She comes with worker's faithfulness
to sow and reap and spin.
She bends her back in common task
to gather harvest in.

She comes with artist's joyfulness
to make and shape and sing.
She gives her hands and from them grows
a free and lovely thing.

She comes, a child in humbleness,
and trust is in her eyes.
And through them, all of life appears
in wondering surprise.

She comes with sister's carefulness
strong to support and bind.
Her voice will speak for justice' sake
and peace is in her mind.

She comes with power like the night
and glory like the day.
Her reign is in the heart of things -
Oh come to us and stay.

Kathryn Galloway b. 1952

GOLDEN THREAD 75.76.

David Dawson, b.1939

1.Shin - ing through the un - i - verse runs the gold - en thread; wo - ven in a - long with white, black, yel - low, green and red_____ gold.

vv.1-4 v.5

Music © David Dawson 2009. Used by permission.

142 Shining through the universe

Shining through the universe
runs the golden thread;
woven in along with white,
black, yellow, green and red.

Cooling water, burning fire,
metal, wood and clay,
in the earth's five elements
the gold thread marks the Way.

If we try to pick it out
from the fabric fair;
when the threads are pulled apart
the gold's no longer there.

Under heaven, over earth,
north to southern pole,
if you trace the golden thread
the Way will calm your soul.

"Turn your feet along the Way",
sages taught of old;
live life well and tread the path
marked by the thread of gold.

Roger Mason b. 1941 based on the Tao Te Ching

LOBE DEN HERREN 14.14.4.7.8.

Stralsund Gesangbuch, 1665

143 Sing for God's glory

Sing for God's glory that colours the dawn of creation,
racing across the sky, trailing bright clouds of elation;
sun of delight
succeeds the velvet of night,
warming the earth's exultation.

Sing for God's power that shatters the chains that would bind us,
searing the darkness of fear and despair that could blind us,
touching our shame
with love that will not lay blame,
reaching out gently to find us.

Sing for God's justice disturbing each easy illusion,
tearing down tyrants and putting our pride to confusion;
life blood of right,
resisting evil and slight,
offering freedom's transfusion.

Sing for God's saints who have travelled faith's journey before us,
who in our weariness give us their hope to restore us;
in them we see
the new creation to be,
spirit of love made flesh for us.

Kathryn Galloway b. 1952

CRUCIFER 10.10.+ Refrain

Sydney Hugo Nicholson, 1875-1947

Refrain

Sing, sing for joy,___ our voi - ces loud we raise, and
join to of - fer now ___ our thank - ful praise.

v.1. Hope makes us strong to see through to the end that
work our___ spi - rits yearn to com - pre - hend.

144 Sing, sing for joy

Sing, sing for joy, our voices loud we raise
and join to offer now our thankful praise.

Hope makes us strong to see through to the end
that work our spirits yearn to comprehend.
Sing, sing for joy, our voices loud we raise
and join to offer now our thankful praise.

Hearts, minds and hands are needed for the task;
to build a peaceful world is all we ask.
Sing, sing for joy, our voices loud we raise
and join to offer now our thankful praise.

'Swords into ploughshares' is our vision clear;
one world our dream; the miracle is near.
Sing, sing for joy, our voices loud we raise
and join to offer now our thankful praise.

Happy are we when we leave fear behind
and share our wealth to serve all humankind.
Sing, sing for joy, our voices loud we raise
and join to offer now our thankful praise.

Peter Sampson b. 1938

AR HYD Y NOS 84.84.88.84.

Welsh Traditional Melody

145 Sleep, my child

Sleep, my child, and peace attend you,
all through the night.
I who love you shall be near you,
all through the night.
Soft the drowsy hours are creeping,
hill and vale in slumber sleeping,
I my loving vigil keeping,
all through the night.

Mother, I can feel you near me,
all through the night.
Father, I know you can hear me,
all through the night.
And when I am your age nearly,
still I will remember clearly,
how you sang and held me dearly,
all through the night.

While the moon her watch is keeping,
all through the night;
while one-half the world is sleeping,
all through the night.
Even while the sun comes stealing,
visions of the day revealing,
breathes a pure and holy feeling,
all through the night.

Alicia S. Carpenter b. 1930

REGENT SQUARE 87.87.87.

Henry Smart, 1813-1879

Note: This tune is printed at No.17 a semitone lower in A Major.

146 Speaking truth in love

Speaking truth in love, we gather
to embrace the unity
of earth's living systems, whirling
towards God's perfect liberty;
reason guided, conscience lighted,
tempered with humility.

Speaking, one unto another,
that which honours highest worth,
and which for ourselves and others
nurtures common life from birth;
just, sustaining, fair society
through the length and breadth of earth.

Speaking peace across this planet
where all living things depend,
each on each, as with our neighbours,
their diversity transcend.
Honour prophets, honour Jesus,
those who welcome God as friend.

Andrew McKean Hill b. 1942

LEAVING OF LISMORE

Traditional Scottish Melody
Arr. David Dawson

1.Spi-rit of earth, root, stone and tree, wa-ter of life, flow-ing in me, keep-ing me sta-ble, nour-ish-ing me, O fill me with liv-ing en-er-gy!

Chorus

Spi-rit of na-ture, heal-ing and free, spi-rit of love, ex-pand-ing in me, spi-rit of life, breathe deep-ly in me, in-spire me with liv-ing en-er-gy!

Note: The guitar chords do not simply replicate the keyboard harmonies- use either or.

147 Spirit of earth, root, stone and tree

Spirit of earth, root, stone and tree,
water of life, flowing in me,
keeping me stable, nourishing me,
O fill me with living energy!
Spirit of nature, healing and free,
spirit of love, expanding in me,
spirit of life, breathe deeply in me,
inspire me with living energy!

Spirit of love, softly draw near,
open my heart, lessen my fear,
sing of compassion, help me to hear,
O fill me with loving energy!
Spirit of nature, healing and free,
spirit of love, expanding in me,
spirit of life, breathe deeply in me,
inspire me with living energy!

Spirit of life, you are my song,
sing in my soul, all my life long,
gladden and guide me, keep me from wrong,
O fill me with sacred energy!
Spirit of nature, healing and free,
spirit of love, expanding in me,
spirit of life, breathe deeply in me,
inspire me with living energy!

Lyanne Mitchell

148 Spirit of Life, come unto me

SPIRIT OF LIFE

Carolyn McDade, b.1935
Arr. David Dawson

Spi - rit of Life, come un - to me.

Sing in my heart all the stir - rings of com - pas - sion.

Blow in the wind, rise in the sea;

move in the hand, giv-ing life the shape of jus - tice.

Roots hold me close; wings set me free;

Spi - rit of Life, come to me, come to me.

Spirit of Life, come unto me.
Sing in my heart all the stirrings of compassion.
Blow in the wind, rise in the sea;
move in the hand, giving life the shape of justice.
Roots hold me close; wings set me free;
Spirit of Life, come to me, come to me.

Words: Carolyn McDade b.1935

QUEM PASTORES LAUDAVERE 88.87.

Melody : 14th century German
Harm. Ralph Vaughan Williams,
1872-1958

1.Still - ness reigns, the winds are sleep - ing. All__ the world__ is bent on keep - ing tryst with night, whose wings are sweep - ing from the west__ each ray__ of light.

149 Stillness reigns

Stillness reigns, the winds are sleeping.
All the world is bent on keeping
tryst with night, whose wings are sweeping
from the west each ray of light.

Dusk, a soft and silken cover,
over all is seen to hover
in its readiness to cover
all the drowsy world, good night.

Those who laboured long, untiring,
hail this time of rest, desiring
strength renewed through sweet retiring,
welcome thoughts of peaceful night;

and through spaces real or seeming
find the Eden of their dreaming,
soar to starry ways, redeeming
hours of toil and pain, good night.

Guttormur J. Guttormsson

LIEBSTER JESU 78.78.88.

Melody : Johann Rudolph Ahle, 1625-1673
Harmonised: Johann Sebastian Bach, 1685-1750

1.Still - ness, creep - ing through this place, soft - ly come and gent - ly hold us; here, a - part from ur - ban race your quiet calm - ness be a - mong us. May we rest with - in your calm - ness; rest be - side you, qui - et still - ness.

150 Stillness, creeping through this place

Stillness, creeping through this place,
softly come and gently hold us;
here, apart from urban race
your quiet calmness be among us.
May we rest within your calmness;
rest beside you, quiet stillness.

Silence, spreading all around,
quietly seeping in between us;
here, away from city sound
with your peacefulness enfold us.
May we feel and trust your presence,
know your peace, deep healing silence.

Spirit, moving through this space,
weaving in and out among us;
here, your pattern brings new grace,
with your breathing, life endow us.
May we your first breath inherit,
feel your breathing, primal spirit.

Andrew McKean Hill b. 1942

BIDDULPH 87.87.

Alan J. T. Myerscough

1.Strong and stead - fast, heart af - firm - ing, clear minds set on sure re - solve– what a life do we in - her - it, what a world is ours___ to own.

Music © Alan J. T. Myerscough 2009. Used by permission.

151 Strong and steadfast

Strong and steadfast, heart-affirming,
clear minds set on sure resolve -
what a life do we inherit,
what a world is ours to own.

Friends and lovers, joyful workers
in a common enterprise,
share the future of our planet;
never can we fail the trust.

Brothers, sisters, mothers, fathers -
God by any other name -
how can we not keep our promise
to each other to be true!

Much there is now to endeavour.
Stir our will to seek the way.
God of peace and God of justice,
yours will be our glorious day.

Peter Sampson b. 1938

TRANSYLVANIA L.M.

16th C. Hungarian Melody

1.Thanks be for these, life's ho - ly times,

mo - ments of grief, days of de - light;

tri - umph and fail - ure in - ter - twine,

shap - ing our vi - sion of the right.

152 Thanks be for these

Thanks be for these, life's holy times,
moments of grief, days of delight;
triumph and failure intertwine,
shaping our vision of the right.

Thanks be for these, for birth and death,
life in between with meaning full;
holy becomes the quickened breath;
we celebrate life's interval.

Thanks be for these, ennobling art,
images welcome to our sight,
music caressing ear and heart,
inviting us to loftier height.

Thanks be for these, who question why,
who noble motives do obey,
those who know how to live and die,
comrades who share this holy way.

Thanks be for these, we celebrate,
sing and rejoice, our trust declare;
press all our faith into our fate;
bless now the destiny we share.

*Richard Seward Gilbert b. 1936 and Joyce Timmerman Gilbert b.
1936*

PASSION CHORALE 76.76.D.

Hans Leo Hassler, 1564-1612
Har. Johann Sebastian Bach, 1685-1750

153 The April Fool has chosen

The April Fool has chosen
to walk the harder way,
no longer in that country
where happy families stay;
no longer by the lakeside
enjoying freedom's breath,
but toward the holy mountain
and enemies and death.

He goes into a city
where angels fear to tread,
his word perhaps to waken
the living from the dead;
then, foolish in the temple,
his deeds of daring bring
to priest and Roman ruler
the danger of a king.

The April Fool has ended
upon a gallows tree;
no help has come from heaven
to loose or set him free;
he dies there, God-forsaken;
he shares our fate and loss,
that we may know God's wisdom -
the folly of the cross.

John Bunyan

Written for the years when Holy Week & Easter include April 1st, All Fools Day.
"The foolishness of God is wiser than men; and the weakness of God is stronger
than men." I Corinthians 1.25

THE BRIGHT WIND OF HEAVEN 12.11.12.11.

John Maynard, 1925-1985

1.The bright wind is blow-ing, the bright wind of heav-en, and where it is go-ing to, no one can say; but— where it is pass-ing our— hearts are a-wak-ing to stretch from the dark-ness and reach for the day.

154 The bright wind is blowing

The bright wind is blowing, the bright wind of heaven,
and where it is going to, no one can say;
but where it is passing our hearts are awaking
to stretch from the darkness and reach for the day.

The bright wind is blowing, the bright wind of heaven,
and many old thoughts will be winnowed away;
the husk that is blown is the chaff of our hating,
the seed that is left is the hope for our day.

The bright wind is blowing, the bright wind of heaven,
the love that it kindles will never betray;
the fire that it fans is the warmth of our caring,
so lean on the wind — it will show us the way.

Cecily Taylor b. 1930

TALLIS' CANON L.M.

Thomas Tallis, c.1505-1585

306

155 The day will come, must come, and soon

The day will come, must come, and soon,
when we will sing a song of joy
with sisters, brothers, not like us,
who share the image of one God.

Whatever name, whichever faith,
at heart we share a common bond,
a shared humanity in God,
whose name and character is love.

That love will drive us to the day
when every wall is broken down,
when love and joy and song are one:
that day will come, must come, and soon.

Andrew Pratt b. 1948

ST. DENIO 11.11.11.11.

Welsh Hymn Melody

156 The earth is the Lord's

'The earth is the Lord's and the fullness thereof.'
Creation reminds us, O God, of your love.
By grace, we are learning; as year leads to year
we're called to be stewards, your caretakers here.

Your rainforests nurture the world that we share;
your wetlands give animals shelter and care;
your coral reefs cradle the life of the sea;
you've shown us, in love, what your good world can be.

Too often, O God, we abuse your good earth
and fail to remember its beauty and worth.
We take from creation much more than we need
and threaten your world through indifference and greed.

May we be good stewards of all that you give,
protecting creation wherever we live.
May we be a church that renews and restores
and lovingly cares for this earth that is yours.

Carolyn Winfrey Gillette.

DUNDEE C.M.

Scottish Psalter, 1615

157 The flame of truth and flame of love

The flame of truth and flame of love
we need both – you and I –
the one will show us how to go,
the other tell us why.

When first this flame of light was lit
above the great abyss,
the truth became a garden, fair,
and love became a kiss.

The earth before the altar kneeled
and heaven with her stood,
for God and light had made them one
and said that all was good.

I bear the flame of truth and love
now as I walk along;
I hold it forth in words and deeds
and fan it with a song.

This borrowed torch of truth and love -
the light of liberty,
I want to pass it on to you
as it was passed to me.

D. Elwyn Davies 1927-1997

MORNING LIGHT 76.76.D.

George James Webb, 1803-1887

158 The flame of truth is kindled

The flame of truth is kindled,
our chalice burning bright;
amongst us moves the Spirit
in whom we take delight.
We worship here in freedom
with conscience unconstrained,
a pilgrim people thankful
for what great souls have gained.

The flame of thought is kindled,
we celebrate the mind;
its search for deepest meaning
that time-bound creeds can't bind.
We celebrate its oneness
with body and with soul,
with universal process,
with God who makes us whole.

The flame of love is kindled,
we open wide our hearts,
that it may burn within us,
fuel us to do our parts.
Community needs building,
a Commonwealth of Earth,
we ask for strength to build it -
a new world come to birth.

Clifford Martin Reed b. 1947

THE FLIGHT OF THE EARLS C.M.D.

Irish Traditional Melody
Arr. David Dawson

1.The green grass brings the air to life up - on this earth - ly globe;
all liv - ing and all grow-ing things are clothed in na - ture's robe.
Hope for the world, hope for our lives grows in God's wil - der - ness!
so for - est, jun -gle, marsh and moor we'll treat with gen -tle - ness.

159 The green grass brings the air to life

1st verse with the music

The green earth yields sufficiently
for every human need
but not enough when human life
is marred by wanton greed;
for each and every one is part
of a much greater whole
the many and the one which make
the universal soul.

The green peace dwells with planet earth
when inner spirits rise
to meet the outer world and build
one home beneath the skies.
Within the garden home of earth
there grows a gracious tree,
whose healing leaves the nations calm
and set their subjects free.

Andrew McKean Hill b. 1942

1. "In God's wilderness lies the hope of the world" [John Muir, Scottish-born
conservationist who founded the Yosemite National Park in California]
2. "The world has enough for everyone's need, but not enough for everyone's greed"
(attributed to Gandhi)
3. "The leaves of the tree were for the healing of the nations" [Revelation 22:2]

SUNSET 98.98.

George Gilbert Stocks, 1877-1960

1.The high-est good-ness is like wa-ter and which by name 'Great Way' we call, finds all the plac-es which we can't reach and with-out ef-fort wa-ters all.

160 The highest goodness

The highest goodness is like water
and which by name 'Great Way' we call,
finds all the places which we can't reach
and without effort waters all.

All plants and fruits and crops are needful;
as also is our staple grain
of showers, of water and of monsoon
which fall on fields from clouds of rain.

But sometimes rains are not forthcoming
and life on earth seems strangely cursed;
so may we manage water fairly
and learn to put the green earth first.

Water at times can seem all powerful
when shook by earth and beat by wind;
in hurricane and wild tsunami
it damages our living kind.

Water is also gentle, healing;
it cools parched throats and bathes sore wounds;
washes our bodies and our raiment,
makes gurgling noise and lapping sounds.

Great Way, we recognize your patterns
and try to puzzle out your ways.
May gentleness and power together
be guiding waymarks for our days.

Andrew McKean Hill b. 1942 (based on the Tao Te Ching)

DICKINSON COLLEGE L.M.

Lee Hastings Bristol Jr., 1923-1979

1.The hu - man touch can light the flame which gives a
bright - ness to the day; the spir - it us - es mor - tal
flame, life's ve - hi - cle for work and play.

161 The human touch

The human touch can light the flame
which gives a brightness to the day;
the spirit uses mortal flame,
life's vehicle for work and play.

The lover's kiss, the friend's embrace,
the clasp of hands to show we care,
the light of welcome on the face
are treasured moments all can share.

May all who come within our reach
be kindled by our inner glow;
not just in spirit's words we preach,
in human touch love's faith we show.

John Andrew Storey, 1935–1997

162 The leaf unfurling

LAYING DOWN 10.10.10.4.

John L. Bell, b.1949

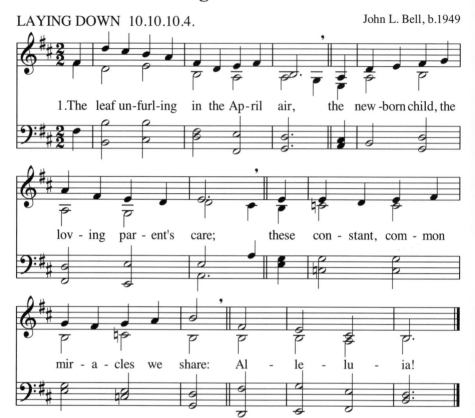

1.The leaf un-furl-ing in the Ap-ril air, the new-born child, the lov-ing par-ent's care; these con-stant, com-mon mir-a-cles we share: Al - le - lu - ia!

1st verse printed with the music

All life is one, a single branching tree,
all pain a part of human misery,
all happiness a gift to you and me:
Alleluia!

The self same bells for joy and sorrow ring.
No one can know what the next hour will bring.
We cry, we laugh, we mourn, and still we sing:
Alleluia!

Don Cohen b.1946

163 The peace of the earth be with you

LA PAZ DE LA TERRE

Traditional Guatemalan Melody
Arr. John L. Bell

The peace of the earth be with you, the
peace of the heav - ens too; the peace of the riv - ers
be with you, the peace of the oc - eans too.

Deep - peace fall-ing ov - er you.
God's - peace grow - ing in you.

Deep___ peace, deep peace fall-ing ov - er you.
God's___ peace, God's peace grow - ing in you.

Original Spanish words translated by Christine Carson

© 1998 WGRG, Iona Commuity, Glasgow G2 3DH. Translation and arrangement used by permission.

SARIE MARAIS C.M.D.

Traditional South African
Arr. David Dawson

1.The se - cret pulse of free-dom throbs in ev- 'ry hu - man heart:

from mar - tyr, mys - tic, her - e - tic, the song of free-dom rang.

The ho - ly day was made for us, not us for ho - ly day;

and hu - man laws should shield from harm, not cage the hu - man heart.

164 The secret pulse of freedom throbs

The secret pulse of freedom throbs
in every human heart:
from martyr, mystic, heretic,
the song of freedom rang.
The holy day was made for us,
not us for holy day;
and human laws should shield from harm,
not cage the human heart.

The sacred rose of love divine
blooms in awakened hearts;
from each to each the answering sign
leaps like enkindled flame.
Love knows no bounds, not even death;
it lightens every hour;
for to all true philosophers
the whole wide earth is home.

When reason sings in harmony
with intuition's tune,
and light the darkness shall embrace
in deep soul alchemy;
then shall the earth with freedom ring
and all her children sing
that love and peace shall be our creed
and banish human greed.

Yvonne Aburrow

1. Jesus : "The Sabbath was made for man, not man for the Sabbath." (Mark 2:27)
2. Giordano Bruno: "Al vero filosofo ogni terreno e patria."

WALK IN THE LIGHT 85.85.+ Refrain

Traditional Melody
Arr. David Dawson

165 The Spirit lives to set us free

The Spirit lives to set us free,
walk, walk in the light.
It binds us all in unity,
walk, walk in the light.
Walk in the light, (3 times) walk in the light of love.

The light that shines is in us all,
walk, walk in the light.
We each must follow our own call,
walk, walk in the light.
Walk in the light, (3 times) walk in the light of love.

Peace begins inside your heart,
walk, walk in the light.
We've got to live it from the start,
walk, walk in the light.
Walk in the light, (3 times) walk in the light of love.

Seek the truth in what you see,
walk, walk in the light.
Then hold it firmly as can be,
walk, walk in the light.
Walk in the light, (3 times) walk in the light of love.

The Spirit lives in you and me,
walk, walk in the light.
Its light will shine for all to see,
walk, walk in the light
Walk in the light, (3 times) walk in the light of love.

Anonymous

THE ROAD AND THE MILES TO DUNDEE 12.11.12.11.

Traditional
Scottish Melody

1.The works of the Lord are cre - a - ted in wis - dom; we
view the earth's won - ders and call him to mind; we
hear what he says in the world we dis - co - ver and
God shows his glo - ry in all that we find.

166 The works of the Lord

The works of the Lord are created in wisdom;
we view the earth's wonders and call him to mind:
we hear what he says in the world we discover
and God shows his glory in all that we find.

Not even the angels have ever been granted
to tell the full story of nature and grace;
but open to God is all human perception,
the mysteries of time and the secrets of space.

The sun every morning lights up his creation,
the moon marks the rhythm of months in their turn;
the glittering stars are arrayed in his honour,
adorning the years as they ceaselessly burn.

The wind is his breath and the clouds are his signal,
the rain and the snow are the robes of his choice;
the storm and the lightning, his watchmen and heralds,
the crash of the thunder, the sound of his voice.

The song is unfinished; how shall we complete it,
and where find the skill to perfect all God's praise?
At work in all places, he cares for all people:
how great is the Lord to the end of all days.

Christopher M. Idle b. 1938 (Ecclesiasticus 42-43)

167 There is a place I call my own

Don Besig
Arr. David Dawson

FLYING FREE 87.87.77.88.

1.There is a place I call my own,_____ where I can
2.But life is not a dis-tant sky_____ with-out a
3.So life's a song that I must sing,_____ a gift of

stand_____ by the sea,_____
cloud,_____ with - out rain,_____
love_____ I must share;

and look be-yond the things I've known_____ and dream that
and I can ne-ver hope that I_____ can tra-vel
and when I see the joy it brings_____ my spi-rits

I_____ might be free._____
on_____ with - out pain._____
soar_____ through the air._____

GENESIS 10.9.10.9.11.10.

Graham Westcott, b.1947

1.Think of a world with-out a-ny flow-ers, think of a world with-out_ a-ny trees, think of a world with-out a-ny sun-shine, think of a world with-out_ a-ny breeze. We thank you, Lord, for flow'rs and trees and sun-shine. We thank you, Lord, and praise your ho-ly name.

168 Think of a world

1st verse is with the music

Think of a world without any animals,
think of a field without any herd,
think of a stream without any fishes,
think of a dawn without any bird.
We thank you, Lord, for all your living creatures.
We thank you, Lord, and praise your holy name.

Think of a world without any paintings,
think of a room where all the walls are bare,
think of a rainbow without any colours,
think of the earth with darkness everywhere.
We thank you, Lord, for paintings and for colours.
We thank you, Lord, and praise your holy name.

Think of a world without any science,
think of a journey with nothing to explore,
think of a quest without any mystery,
nothing to seek and nothing left in store.
We thank you, Lord, for miracles of science,
We thank you, Lord, and praise your holy name.

Think of a world without any people,
think of a street with no-one living there,
think of a town without any houses,
no- one to love and nobody to care.
We thank you, Lord, for families and friendships.
We thank you, Lord, and praise your holy name.

Doreen Newport 1927-2004

331

WOLVERCOTE 76.76.D.

William Harold Ferguson, 1874-1950

169 This day confirms a union

This day confirms a union,
an act of heart and mind,
and we are met to witness
the promises that bind,
a binding that brings freedom
to care and serve and give,
to share in thought and action
that love may grow and live.

This day confirms a union
from which each may gain power
to live a life of courage,
yet tender as a flower:
two lives of peace and passion,
two lives of work and joy
which, joined today before us,
may all that's good employ.

This day confirms a union;
it is a day of hope,
a day to be remembered
when it is hard to cope.
So may these two in good times
and times of trouble prove
that partnerships will triumph,
sustained by holy love.

Peter Galbraith b. 1928

GALAXY C.M.

Michael Dawney

1.This do in me - mo - ry of me; eat now this bro - ken bread. This is my life from death set free, here on my ta - ble spread.

170 This do in memory of me

This do in memory of me;
eat now this broken bread.
This is my life from death set free,
here on my table spread.

This do in memory of me;
drink now this cup, I said.
This shows my love for all to see,
here on my table spread.

We praise your living memory,
remembering all you said.
Your words and life have set us free,
here through your table spread.

Wayne Bradley Robinson b. 1936

171 This is the moment

SOMETHING TO SAY

Words and Music: Myrna Michell, b.1951

This, this is the mo - ment when we go— our se - par-ate ways; there's something to hear,— there's something to draw,— and some-thing to play._____ And this, this is what all_____ of us can of - fer some-one to-

Note: The song was written to mark the point in a service when the children leave for their own activities.

Words and Music © Myrna Michell. Used by permission.

172 This is the truth that passes understanding

DONNE SECOURS 11.10 .11. 10.

Genevan Psalter, 1551

This is the truth that pass-es un-der-stand - ing,
this is the joy to all for-ev - er free:
life springs from death and shat-ters ev -'ry fet - ter,
and win-ter turns to spring e-ter - nal - ly.

Words: Robert Terry Weston 1898-1988

173 Though gathered here to celebrate

DISTANT BELOVED 86.886.

W. Frederick Wooden, b.1953

1. Though ga- thered here to ce - le-brate, my spi - rit's burn-ing low; in - stead of serv - ing, now I wait, the breath of wor -ship's not too late, breathe, let the em- bers glow.

2. There have been loss- es on the way; a par - ent, part - ner, friend. At times I need to grieve and say, "I'll live my life from day to day, be near and help me mend."

3. The still - ness strips the mask a - way, ex - pos - es lone - ly hearts; self - pi - ty must not have its way; I'll live my life from day to day, and now the heal-ing starts.

Christine Doreian Michaels b.1942

MELCOMBE L.M.

Samuel Webbe (the elder), 1740-1816

174 Though I may speak with bravest fire

Though I may speak with bravest fire
and have the gift to all inspire
and have not love, my words are vain
as sounding brass and hopeless gain.

Though I may give all I possess
and striving so my love profess
but not be given by love within,
the profit soon turns strangely thin.

Come, Spirit, come, our hearts control,
our spirits long to be made whole.
Let inward love guide every deed;
by this we worship and are freed.

Hal H. Hopson b. 1933 [1 Corinthians 13:1-3]

BROTHER JAMES'S AIR 86.86.86.

Melody: James L. M. Bain, d. 1925
Arr. David Dawson

175 To seek and find our natural mind

To seek and find our natural mind,
and suffering let go,
awake from night, behold the light,
find every life aglow;
awake from night, behold the light,
find every life aglow.

To seek and find compassion's law
and share the holy quest,
awaken to the cosmic awe,
find peace and be at rest;
awaken to the cosmic awe,
find peace and be at rest.

To seek and find community,
the love that will not cease,
begin today the joyful way,
walking the path of peace;
begin today the joyful way,
walking the path of peace.

Richard Boeke b. 1931

Original version refers to the Buddha (our natural mind), the Dharma
(compassion's law) and the Sangha (community)

John Goss, 1800-1880

176 To sunlit ranges of life's peaks

To sunlit ranges of life's peaks
upward our hearts aspire,
by rock and snow and fields of ice
ascending higher.

Together in this enterprise,
sharing a common hope,
each to the next securely linked
by one firm rope.

Then strength of all is strength of each,
as in the rope's design
with strand each reinforcing strand,
all intertwine.

So reason, passion, comradeship
in faith and hope and love
unite to bind us as we scale
the heights above.

We follow paths once pioneered
by climbers long ago
to vistas over splendid scenes
spread far below.

Phillip Hewett

CHURCH TRIUMPHANT L.M.

James William Elliott, 1833-1915

177 To you who would as pilgrims go

To you who would as pilgrims go
with eager steps and hearts aglow,
when on the holy city bent
be not deterred from high intent.

For people need triumphant days
with ample reassuring praise,
and palms extol while thorns do not -
and none would choose the martyr's lot.

So easy now to join the throng
with flowering branch and palm and song.
So hard to see on such a day
the beggar's hand beside the way.

How fine to do the pleasant deed,
to serve the current favoured need,
but hope needs those who think and choose -
uphold a cause they well may lose.

For those who would as pilgrims go
both scorn and failure well may know,
and high intent can lead to pain
and gifts must never be for gain.

Janet H. Bowering

ST FULBERT C.M.

Henry John Gauntlett, 1805-1876

178 Together now we join as one

Together now we join as one
our common faith to sing;
to render to this pilgrim world
our heartfelt offering.

We strive to be a fellowship
with mind and conscience free,
to search for truth and saving light
in cosmic mystery.

We worship God - love's source and power;
we celebrate the life
that all earth's children freely share
beyond their sinful strife.

We would, in love, serve humankind
with caring, justice, peace;
and with the earth seek harmony
that pride and pillage cease.

We hold in reverence the man
who walked in Galilee,
who healed the sick and loved the poor -
revealed divinity.

We welcome truth, we welcome light,
all prophecy and song,
whoever they be channelled through
to all they shall belong.

Clifford Martin Reed b. 1947

TENDERNESS 5.5.10.D.

Colin Alexander Gibson, b.1933

1.Touch the earth light- ly, use the earth gent - ly, nour -ish the life of the world in our care;__ gift of great won - der, ours to sur- ren - der, trust for the child - ren to - mor - row will bear.__

Note: This tune is printed a semitone higher, in Bb major, at No.139.

179 Touch the earth lightly

Touch the earth lightly,
use the earth gently,
nourish the life of the world in our care;
gift of great wonder,
ours to surrender,
trust for the children tomorrow will bear.

We who endanger,
who create hunger,
agents of death for all creatures that live,
we who would foster
clouds of disaster,
God of our planet, forestall and forgive!

Let there be greening,
birth from the burning,
water that blesses and air that is sweet,
health in God's garden,
hope in God's children,
regeneration that peace will complete.

God of all living,
God of all loving,
God of the seedling, the snow and the sun,
teach us, deflect us,
Christ re-connect us,
using us gently and making us one.

Shirley Erena Murray b. 1931

YARNBURY 87.87.7.

David Dawson, b.1939

1.View the star - ry realm of heav - en, shin- ing dis - tant em - pires sing. Sky - song of —— cel - es - tial child - ren turns each win - ter in - to spring, turns each win - ter in - to spring.

180 View the starry realm of heaven

View the starry realm of heaven,
shining distant empires sing.
Skysong of celestial children
turns each winter into spring,
turns each winter into spring.

Great you are, beyond conception,
God of gods and God of stars.
My soul soars with your perception,
I escape from prison bars,
I escape from prison bars.

You, the one within, all forming
in my heart and mind and breath,
you my guide through hate's fierce storming,
courage in both life and death,
courage in both life and death.

Life is yours, in you I prosper,
seed will come to fruit I know.
Trust that after winter's snowfall
walls will melt and truth will flow,
walls will melt and truth will flow.

Norbert Capek 1870-1942
ET Paul and Anita Munk and Richard Boeke b. 1931

TOBY 10.10.10.10. Dactylic

Barry Brown

1. Wake, now, my sens - es, and hear the earth call;
feel the deep pow - er of be - ing in all;
keep with the web of cre - a - tion your vow,
giv - ing, re - ceiv - ing as love shows us how.

Music © Barry Brown 2009. Used by permission.

181 Wake, now, my senses

Wake, now, my senses, and hear the earth call;
feel the deep power of being in all;
keep with the web of creation your vow,
giving, receiving as love shows us how.

Wake, now, my reason, reach out to the new;
join with each pilgrim who quests for the true;
honour the beauty and wisdom of time;
suffer thy limit, and praise the sublime.

Wake, now, compassion, give heed to the cry;
voices of suffering fill the wide sky;
take as your neighbour both stranger and friend,
praying and striving their hardship to end.

Wake, now, my conscience, with justice thy guide;
join with all people whose rights are denied;
take not for granted a privileged place;
God's love embraces the whole human race.

Wake, now, my vision of ministry clear;
brighten my pathway with radiance here;
mingle my calling with all who would share;
work toward a planet transformed by our care.

Thomas J. S. Mikelson, b. 1936

SINGING FOR OUR LIVES

Holly Near, b.1944
Arr. David Dawson

1. We are a gen-tle, an-gry peo_____ ple, and we are sing-ing, sing-ing for_ our lives._____

We are a gen-tle, ang-ry peo_____ ple, and we are sing-ing, sing-ing for_ our lives._____

182 We are a gentle angry people

We are a gentle, angry people,
and we are singing, singing for our lives.
We are a gentle, angry people,
and we are singing, singing for our lives.

We are a justice seeking people,
and we are singing, singing for our lives.
We are a justice seeking people,
and we are singing, singing for our lives.

We are young and old together,
and we are singing, singing for our lives.
We are young and old together,
and we are singing, singing for our lives.

We are a land of many colours,
and we are singing, singing for our lives.
We are a land of many colours,
and we are singing, singing for our lives.

We are gay and straight together,
and we are singing, singing for our lives.
We are gay and straight together,
and we are singing, singing for our lives.

We are a gentle, loving people,
and we are singing, singing for our lives.
We are a gentle, loving people,
and we are singing, singing for our lives.

Holly Near b. 1944

Words © Hereford Press Hereford Music. 1222 Preservation Park Way, Oakland, CA 94612 Tel: (510) 286-7971; FAX: 510 835-1459

SPINNERS AND WEAVERS

Heather Lynn Hanson

1.We are daugh - ters of the *stars,* we are sons of the
earth; we are *spin - ners* and *wea - vers* in this web of
life; and the *joy* that we weave reach - es out be - yond the
stars and deep with - in the cen - tre of our be - ing.

Note: This is a zipper song. 'Zip' in your own words, instead of the bold italicised words, to create verses of your own.

Music © Heather Lynn Hanson 2005. Used by permission.

183 We are daughters of the stars

We are daughters of the stars, we are sons of the earth;
we are spinners and weavers in this web of life;
and the joy that we weave reaches out beyond the stars
and deep within the centre of our being.

We are daughters of the orchards, we are sons of the field;
we are planters and reapers in this web of life;
and the vision that we weave reaches out beyond the stars
and deep within the centre of our being.

We are daughters of tomorrow, we are sons of our dreams;
we are planners and builders in this web of life;
and the future that we weave reaches out beyond the stars
and deep within the centre of our being.

Heather Lynn Hanson

GLENFINLAS 65.65.

Kenneth G. Finlay, 1882-1974

Music © Broomhill Church of Scotland, Glasgow.

184 We are here in stillness

We are here in stillness,
we are here in prayer,
we are here in silence
nothing can compare.

We are here rejoicing,
we are here for praise,
we are here delighting
all our livelong days.

We are here to ponder,
we are here to pause,
we are here for wonder,
marvel and applause.

Andrew McKean Hill b. 1942

185 We are marching in the light of God

SIYAHAMBA

South African Melody
Arr. Anders Nyberg

* Note: Replace 'marching' with other words: singing, dancing, walking etc.

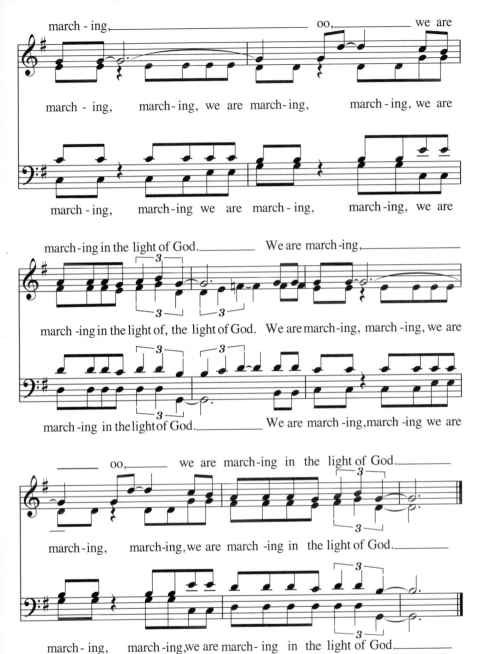

English translation from Xhosa words by Anders Nyberg

Music © 1990 Wild Goose Publications, Iona Community, Glasgow G2 3DH. Used by permission

363

ASCENSION

Henry Hugh Bancroft, 1904-1988

1. We are trav-'llers on a jour-ney which brought us from the sun,
when pri-mal star ex-plo-ded and earth in or-bit spun;
but now as hu-man dwell-ers up-on earth-pla-net's crust,
we strive for liv-ing sys-tems whose ways are kind and just.

186 We are travellers on a journey

We are travellers on a journey
which brought us from the sun,
when primal star exploded
and earth in orbit spun;
but now as human dwellers
upon earth-planet's crust,
we strive for living systems
whose ways are kind and just.

We are travellers on a journey
which grows from human seed,
and through our birth and childhood
goes where life's path may lead;
but now we are delving deeper
in quest of greater worth
and reaching unknown regions
and planets of new birth.

We are travellers on a journey
through realms of inner space
where joy and peace are planets
that circle stars of grace;
and when we find the stillness
which comes at journey's end,
there'll be complete refreshment,
a resting place, a friend.

Andrew McKean Hill b. 1942

PILGRIMS' HYMN

Donald Swann, 1923-1994

1. We ask that we live and we la-bour in peace, in peace; that all shall be our neigh-bours in peace, in peace; dis-trust and ha-tred will turn to love, all the pris- 'ners freed, and our on-ly war will be the one a-gainst all hu - man need.

187 We ask that we live . . . in peace

We ask that we live and we labour in peace, in peace;
that all shall be our neighbours in peace, in peace;
distrust and hatred will turn to love,
all the prisoners freed,
and our only war will be the one
against all human need.

We work for the end of disunion in truth, in truth;
that all may be one in communion in truth, in truth;
we choose the road of peace and prayer
countless pilgrims trod,
so that Hindu, Muslim, Christian, Jew
are together in God.

We call to our sisters and brothers, unite, unite!
that all may live for others, unite, unite!
and so the nations will be as one,
one the flag unfurled,
one law, one life, one hope, one goal,
one people and one world.

Donald Swann 1923-1994

Words and Music © Stainer & Bell Ltd, 23 Gruneisen Road, London N3 1DZ.
www.stainer.co.uk Used by permission.

TO GOD BE THE GLORY 11.11.11.11.+ Refrain William H. Doane,1836-1906

188 We bring to the altar

We bring to the altar the bread of our toil,
the food that sustains us, from sea and from soil.
We offer our thanks for the bounties in store,
and pray that the whole world may share in them more.
Gather in, gather in, may we riches enjoy,
gather in, gather in, and our voices employ,
to sing to our maker the hymn of our praise,
for all that life offers in so many ways.

We bring to the altar the work we have done,
the coal we have mined and the yarn we have spun.
May all have the warmth and the clothing they need,
and so may our labours bring blessings indeed.
Gather in, gather in, may we riches enjoy,
gather in, gather in, and our voices employ,
to sing to our maker the hymn of our praise,
for all that life offers in so many ways.

We bring to the altar those whom we love best,
who stand by us daily, by whom we are blessed.
We offer our thanks for the gifts of true love,
the human affections the angels approve.
Gather in, gather in, may we riches enjoy,
gather in, gather in, and our voices employ,
to sing to our maker the hymn of our praise,
for all that life offers in so many ways.

David Andrew Usher

CHRISTUS DER IST MEIN LEBEN C.M.

Melchior Vulpius, c.1560-1616

1.We cel - e - brate the web of life, its mag - ni - tude we sing; for we can see di - vin - i - ty in ev - 'ry liv - ing thing.

189 We celebrate the web of life

We celebrate the web of life,
its magnitude we sing;
for we can see divinity
in every living thing.

A fragment of the perfect whole
in cactus and in quail,
as much in tiny barnacle
as in the great blue whale.

Of ancient dreams we are the sum;
our bones link stone to star,
and bind our future worlds to come
with worlds that were and are.

Respect the water, land, and air
which gave all creatures birth;
protect the lives of all that share
the glory of the earth.

Alicia S. Carpenter b. 1930

Charles Hubert Hastings Parry, 1848-1918

Note: This is a simpler arrangment of the original harmonisation.
The more traditional arrangement can be found in many hymnals.

190 We come, dear Lord, to celebrate

We come, dear Lord, to celebrate
the love our friends have found;
and thank you, God, for their embrace,
the joy and promise in this place
which makes it holy ground,
which makes it holy ground.

Help them fulfil the vows made here;
let this new family share
a welcome home, a future blessed
by love and laughter, grace and guest,
with time enough to spare,
to listen, love, and care.

In seeking what the future holds,
in letting go the past,
we seek your grace to clear a way
through what must go and what should stay
if love is meant to last,
if love is meant to last.

John L. Bell b. 1949

Words © WGRG (Wild Goose Resource Group) Pearce Institute,
840 Govan Rd, Glasgow, G51 3UU; Tel: 0141 445 4561 Fax: 0141 445 4295

WOODLANDS 10.10.10.10.

Walter Greatorex, 1877-1949

Note: This tune is printed a tone lower, in C Major, at Number 196

191 We have a dream

We have a dream: this nation will arise,
and truly live according to its creed,
that all are equal in their maker's eyes,
and none shall suffer through another's greed.

We have a dream that one day we shall see
a world of justice, truth and equity,
where sons of slaves and daughters of the free
will share the banquet of community.

We have a dream of deserts brought to flower,
once made infertile by oppression's heat,
when love and truth shall end oppressive power,
and streams of righteousness and justice meet.

We have a dream: our children shall be free
from judgements based on colour or on race;
free to become whatever they may be,
of their own choosing in the light of grace.

We have a dream that truth will overcome
the fear and anger of our present day;
that black and white will share a common home,
and hand in hand will walk the pilgrim way.

We have a dream: each valley will be raised,
and every mountain, every hill, brought down;
then shall creation echo perfect praise,
and share God's glory under freedom's crown!

Michael Forster based on speech by Martin Luther King jr.

Donna Kasbohm

Refrain

We have la-boured, and we have baked the bread,
we have wo-ven cloth; we have nur-tured life. Now we're weav-ing a

Fine

new cre-a-tion too. Praise, O - God, all - praise to you!

Verses

1. God of sim-ple com-mon things, God of cloth and bread,

D.C.

help us mend our tat-tered lives; Spir-it be the thread.

192 We have laboured

We have laboured, and we have baked the bread,
We have woven cloth; we have nurtured life.
Now we're weaving a new creation too.
Praise, O God, all praise to you!

God of simple common things,
God of cloth and bread,
help us mend our tattered lives;
Spirit be the thread. *Refrain*

As we change our daily lives,
justice is our call;
safer homes and city streets
bread and drink for all. *Refrain*

Weave our frayed and varied strands,
shaping one design.
May our colours richly blend,
as our lives entwine. *Refrain*

Clothed in wisdom may we live,
robed in love and praise.
May our labour turn to joy,
as we learn your ways.

We have laboured, and we have baked the bread,
We have woven cloth; we have nurtured life.
Now we're weaving a new creation too.
Praise, O God, all praise to you!

Ruth C. Duck b. 1947

193 We laugh, we cry

Words and Music:
Shelley Jackson Denham, b.1950

CREDO

1. We laugh, we cry, we live, we die, we dance, we sing our song. We need to feel there's some-thing here to which we can be-long. We need to feel the free-dom just to have some time a-lone. But most of all we need close friends we can call our ve-ry own.

2. A child is born a-mongst us and we feel a spec-ial glow. We see time's end-less jour-ney as we watch the ba-by grow. We thrill to hear i-mag-in-a-tion free-ly run-ning wild. We de-di-cate our minds and hearts to the spi-rit of the child.

3. Our lives are full of won-der and our time is ve-ry brief. The death of one a-mongst us fills us all with pain and grief. But as we live, so shall we die, and when our lives are done the mem-or-ies we shared with friends, they will lin-ger on and on.

4. We seek e-lu-sive ans-wers to the ques-tions of this life. We seek to put an end to all the waste of hu-man strife. We search for truth, e-qual-i-ty, and bless-ed peace of mind. And then we come to-geth-er here, to make sense of what we find.

own. And we be-lieve in life, and in the strength_____ of
child. And we be-lieve in life, and in the strength_____ of
on. And we be-lieve in life, and in the strength_____ of
find. And we be-lieve in life, and in the strength_____ of

love, and we have found a need to be to-ge - ther._____
love, and we have found a time to be to-ge - ther._____
love; and we have found a place to be to-ge - ther._____
love; and we have found a joy to be to-ge - ther._____

——— We have our hearts to give, we have our thoughts to re-
——— And with the grace of age, we share the won - der of
——— We have the right to grow, we have the gift to be-
——— And in our search for peace, may-be we'll fi - nal-ly

ceive, and we be-lieve that shar-ing is an ans - wer.
youth, and we be-lieve that grow-ing is an ans - wer.
lieve that peace with-in our liv-ing is an ans - wer.
see: e - ven to ques-tion tru-ly is an ans - wer.

BEAMSLEY 11.10.11.10.11.10.

David Dawson, b.1939

1.We light the flame that kin-dles our de-vo-tions. We lift our
hearts in blessed com-mu-ni-ty. The mind has thoughts, the
heart its true e-mo-tions, we cel-e-brate in wor-ship, full and
free. Our faith tran-scends the boun-da-ries of
oc-eans. All shall be grant-ed worth and dig-ni-ty.

194 We light the flame

We light the flame that kindles our devotions.
We lift our hearts in blessed community.
The mind has thoughts, the heart its true emotions,
we celebrate in worship, full and free.
Our faith transcends the boundaries of oceans.
All shall be granted worth and dignity.

So many ways to witness to the wonder.
So many dreams by day for us to dare.
Yet, reaching out, each way is made the grander,
and love made bold for dreamers everywhere.
Diversity will never cast asunder
our common weal, our bonds of mutual care.

Infinite Spirit, dwell with us, we pray thee,
that we may share in life abundantly.
Forgive our sins, feed us with good bread daily,
with strength resist temptation steadfastly.
O God of life, sustain us now, and may we
with mindful hearts, be thankful constantly.

David Andrew Usher

SURSUM CORDA 10.10.10.10.

Alfred Morton Smith, 1879-1971

1.We sing a love that sets all peo-ple free,

that blows like wind, that burns like scorch-ing flame,

en-folds the earth, springs up like wa-ter clear.

Come, liv-ing love, live in our hearts to - day.

195 We sing a love

We sing a love that sets all people free,
that blows like wind, that burns like scorching flame,
enfolds the earth, springs up like water clear.
Come, living love, live in our hearts today.

We sing a love that seeks another's good,
that longs to serve and not to count the cost,
a love that yielding finds itself made new.
Come, caring love, live in our hearts today.

We sing a love, unflinching, unafraid
to be itself despite another's wrath,
a love that stands alone and undismayed.
Come, strengthening love, live in our hearts today.

We sing a love, that wandering will not rest
until it finds its way, its home, its source,
through joy and sadness pressing on refreshed.
Come, pilgrim love, live in our hearts today.

We sing the Holy Spirit, full of love,
who seeks out scars of ancient bitterness,
brings to our wounds the healing grace of Christ.
Come, radiant love, live in our hearts today.

June Boyce-Tillman b. 1943

WOODLANDS 10.10.10.10.

Walter Greatorex, 1877-1949

Note: This tune is printed a tone higher, in D Major, at Number 191

196 We sing the faith

We sing the faith, which gives us confidence
for human dwelling in the vast immense
and finding there within the great unknown
that there's a cosmic law and order shown.

We sing the hope, which shows us there are ways
for living through our very darkest days
and glimpse beyond a path which leads us on
to find the place where new days have begun.

We sing the love, which is creation's law,
and in a single whole its parts will draw;
and since parts turn and swerve, collide and move,
forgiveness is the final form of love.

Faith, hope and love: we honour each and three
but there's one virtue which we all agree
stands out among the others far above
and that 'the greatest of the three is love'.

Andrew McKean Hill b. 1942

HORSLEY C.M.

William Horsley, 1774-1858

197 We walk the holy ground of earth

We walk the holy ground of earth
which you, O God, have made,
a jewel in space to be our home,
in velvet darkness laid.

In endless miracle of life
a wondrous web you weave,
and, for creation's tapestry,
your people's thanks receive.

But we have torn its subtle threads,
befouled its colours bright;
our pride has led us to destroy
where wisdom should delight.

We now repent the foolishness
which led us to despoil,
which made us aliens in the world,
though moulded from its soil.

Creator spirit, God of love,
complete what you've begun;
restore our fractured consciousness
that this world may be one.

Clifford Martin Reed b. 1947

198 We'll build a land

Carolyn McDade, b.1935
Arr. Betsy Jo Angebranndt, b.1931

CREATION OF PEACE

1. We'll build a land where we bind up the bro-ken,—
2. We'll build a land where we bring the good ti-dings to
3. We'll build a land build-ing up an-cient cit-ies,—
4. Come, build a land where the man-tles of prai-ses re-

We'll build a land where the cap-tives go free, where the oil of
all the af-flic-ted and all those who mourn. And we'll give them
rais-ing up de-vas-ta-tions of old; re-stor-ing
sound from spir-its once faint and once weak; where like oaks of

glad-ness dis-solves all mourn-ing. O - we'll build a prom-ised
gar-lands in-stead of ash-es. O - we'll build a land where
ru-ins of gen-er-a-tions. O - we'll build a land of
right-eous-ness stand her peo-ple. O - come build the land, my

Chorus

land that can be.
peace - is born.
peo - ple so bold.
peo - ple we seek.

Come build a land__ where sis - ters and bro - thers, a - noin - ted by God__ may then cre - ate peace: where jus - tice shall roll__ down__ like wa - ters, and peace like an ev - er flow - ing stream.

Words: Barbara Zanotti (adapted from Isaiah and Amos)

NOEL NOUVELET 11.11.11.11.

French Carol Tune
Arr. David Dawson

1.Wea - ver God, Cre - a - tor, sets life___ on the loom,

draws out threads of co - lour from prim - or - dial gloom.

v.3

Wise in the de - sign - ing, in the weav - ing deft;

love and jus - tice joined - the fab - ric's___ warp and weft.

Music © Arrangement used by permission.

199 Weaver God, Creator

Weaver God, Creator, sets life on the loom,
draws out threads of colour from primordial gloom.
Wise in the designing, in the weaving deft;
love and justice joined – the fabric's warp and weft.

Called to be co-weavers, yet we break the thread
and may smash the shuttle and the loom, instead.
Careless and greedy, we deny by theft
love and justice joined – the fabric's warp and weft.

Weaver God, great Spirit, may we see your face
tapestried in trees, in waves and winds of space;
tenderness teach us, lest we be bereft
of love and justice joined –– the fabric's warp and weft.

Weavers we are called, yet woven too we're born,
for the web is seamless: if we tear, we're torn.
Gently may we live - that fragile earth be left;
love and justice joined – the fabric's warp and weft.

Kate Compston

DARWALL'S 148th 66.66.88.

J. Darwall, 1731-1789

200 What does the Lord require?

What does the Lord require
for praise and offering?
What sacrifice desire,
or tribute bid us bring?
But only this: true justice do,
love mercy too, and walk with God.

True justice always means
defending of the poor,
the righting of the wrong,
reforming ancient law.
This is the path, true justice do,
love mercy too, and walk with God.

Love mercy and be kind,
befriend, forgive, always,
and welcome all who come
to sing with us in praise:
and in this way, true justice do,
love mercy too, and walk with God.

Yes, humbly walk that way,
free from all pompous pride,
in quiet simplicity,
God always at our side:
thus evermore, true justice do,
love mercy too, and walk with God.

John Bunyan (lines 1 to 4 by A.F.Bayly)

"What doth the Lord require of thee, but to do justly, and to love mercy,
and to walk humbly with thy God" Micah 6.8

DIADEMATA S.M.D.

George J Elvey, 1816-1893

1.What shall we say to them when they all want to know

that God is in the world and_ feels their in-most se-crets glow?

We all must say to them what we all know for sure,

that there's a good-ness in the world which ev - er shall en - dure.

201 What shall we say to them

What shall we say to them
when they all want to know
that God is in the world and feels
their inmost secrets glow?
We all must say to them
what we all know for sure
that there's a goodness in the world
which ever shall endure.

What shall we do for them
when they are in distress
and anguish burns within their hearts
for which they seek redress?
We all must help them live
with confidence and trust
that if we hold fast to the truth
love lights up even dust.

What is our vision bright
which we must show the world:
how perfect love can cast out fear
and life's flag be unfurled?
We may not give up hope;
we will not give up love.
Our lives are grounded in the faith,
in one God we all move.

Peter Sampson b. 1938

English Traditional Melody
Arr. Ralph Vaughan Williams, 1872-1958

202 When earth is changed and waters roar

When earth is changed and waters roar,
and mountains tremble, strong no more,
when tumult floods our lives, our homes,
God, be our help when trouble comes.

When death takes those we love the best,
when illness robs our ease and rest,
O Holy Lover, hold us fast
as long as grief and trouble last.

When answers die on silent lips
and truth slips through our fingertips,
God, stay beside us in our hell,
that we may live the questions well.

God, keep us safe till peace returns
and raised from ashes, new hope burns.
Through change and tumult be our guide.
God, shelter us till storms subside.

Ruth C. Duck b. 1947
incorporating images from Psalm 46 and from Rainer Maria Rilke

ST. COLUMBA 87.87.Iambic

203 When human voices cannot sing

When human voices cannot sing
and human hearts are breaking,
we bring our grief to you, O God,
who knows our inner aching.

Set free our spirits from all fear –
the cloud of dark unknowing,
and let your light pierce through and show
the pathway of our going.

Make real for us your holding love,
the love which is your meaning,
the power to move the stone of death,
to heal us, in our grieving;

and let the one we love now go
where we, in faith will follow,
to travel in the Spirit's peace,
to make an end of sorrow.

Shirley Erena Murray b. 1931

204 When I am frightened

Shelley Jackson Denham, b.1950
Arr. Jeannie Gagné, b.1960

ETHICAL RELATIONS

1. When I am fright-ened, will you re-as-sure me? When I'm un-certain, will you hold my hand? Will you be strong for me, Sing to me qui-et-ly? Will you share

2. When I am ang-ry, will you still em-brace me? When I am thought-less, will you un-der-stand? Will you be-lieve in me, stand by me will-ing-ly? Will you share

3. When I am troub-led, will you lis-ten to me? When I am lone-ly, will you be my friend? Will you be there for me, com-fort me ten-der-ly? Will you share

Words: Shelley Jackson Denham, b.1950

Music and Words © Used by permission. All rights reserved.

CALON LAN 87.87.D.

John Hughes, 1872-1914

205 When I see the purple heather

When I see the purple heather
like a gown upon the hill;
when I see the lark ascending
to the sweetness of its trill;
I'm reminded of the mountain
and the love that will not cease,
of the teacher of God's kingdom
and the angels' song of peace.

When I see the lake reflecting
in its mirror light of day;
when I see in April pastures
sheep that graze and lambs that play;
I'm reminded of the healing
on the shores of Galilee,
and the 'Lord' who 'is my shepherd'
who will lead and comfort me.

When I see the pathway winding
on and on so far ahead;
when I see the river widening
as it flows along its bed:
I can hear a voice proclaiming,
'I'm the way, so do not grieve;
peace I give like flowing waters;
do not fear - my peace I leave'.

D. Elwyn Davies 1927-1997

ENGELBERG 10.10.10.4.

Charles Villiers Stanford, 1852-1924

1.When in our mus - sic God is glo - ri - fied,

— and a - dor - a - tion leaves no room for pride,

— it is as though the whole cre - a - tion cried

vv 1-3
Al - le - lu - ia!

v.4
Al - le - lu - ia!

206 When in our music God is glorified

When in our music God is glorified,
and adoration leaves no room for pride,
it is as though the whole creation cried
Alleluia!

How often, making music, we have found
a new dimension in the world of sound,
as worship moved us to a more profound
Alleluia!

So has the church, in liturgy and song,
in faith and love, through centuries of wrong,
borne witness to the truth in every tongue,
Alleluia!

Let every instrument be tuned for praise!
Let all rejoice who have a voice to raise!
and may God give us faith to sing always
Alleluia!

Frederick Pratt Green 1903-2000

FINLANDIA 11.10.11.10.11.10.

Jean Sibelius, 1865-1957

207 When memory fades

When memory fades and recognition falters,
when eyes we love grow dim and minds confused,
speak to our souls of love that never alters,
speak to our hearts by pain and fear abused.
O God of life and healing peace, empower us
with patient courage, by your grace infused.

As frailness grows, and youthful powers diminish
and weary arms decline in strength and skill,
your ageing servants faithfully shall finish
their earthly tasks, obedient to your will.
We grieve their fading, yet rejoice, believing
your arms, unwearying, will uphold us still.

Within your Spirit, goodness lives unfading;
the past and future mingle into one.
All joys remain, with heavenly light pervading;
no valued deed will ever be undone.
Your mind enfolds all finite acts and offerings;
held in your heart, our deathless life is won!

Mary Louise Bringle b. 1953

208 When our heart is in a holy place

HOLY PLACE

Words and Music: Joyce Poley, b.1941
Arr. Lorne Kellett, b.1950

Chorus
When our heart is in_____ a ho-ly place, when our heart is in a ho-ly place, we are blessed with love and a-maz-ing grace, when our heart is in a ho-ly place.

Last time to Coda

Verses
1.When we
2.When we
3.When we

Words and Music © Songstyle Music (SOCAN). Used by permission.

MENDIP C.M.

English Traditional Melody
Arr. Ralph Vaughan Williams, 1872-1958

209 When sudden terror tears apart

When sudden terror tears apart
the world we thought was ours,
we find how fragile strength can be,
how limited our powers.

As tower and fortress fall, we watch
with disbelieving stare
and numbly hear the anguished cries
that pierce the ash-filled air.

Yet most of all we are aware
of emptiness and void:
of lives cut short, of structures razed,
of confidence destroyed.

From this abyss of doubt and fear
we grope for words to pray,
and hear our stammering tongues embrace
a timeless 'Kyrie'.

Have mercy, Lord, give strength and peace,
and make our courage great;
restrain our urge to seek revenge,
to turn our hurt to hate.

Help us to know your steadfast love,
your presence near as breath;
rekindle in our hearts the hope
of life that conquers death.

Carl Pickens Daw Jr. b. 1944

Charles Crozat Converse, 1832-1918

1.When the song of life is ring - ing through the green fields and the wood

and the love of God is sing - ing in your mind and in your blood,

ho - ly an-gels come to give you won -drous gifts of joy and peace;

and the soul will leap with rap - ture in a dance of glad re - lease.

210 When the song of life is ringing

When the song of life is ringing
through the green fields and the wood
and the love of God is singing
in your mind and in your blood,
holy angels come to give you
wondrous gifts of joy and peace;
and the soul will leap with rapture
in a dance of glad release.

But when life's harsh road has brought us
only hurt and grief and pain
and the darkness hides the promise
we feel now was made in vain,
sad the song we sing amidst tears
from the well of human woe,
for no angels' song the soul hears,
where the heart is stricken low.

Yet in life, if we stay faithful
to the trust we cannot shake,
if we honour our creator
with this life we did not make,
we shall find how God supports us –
God who's true in everything –
brings us through the dark and lean times
to that place where angels sing.

David Charles Doel

PORTENT L.M.

Jillian Bray

1.Where are the voi-ces for the earth?

Where are the eyes to see her pain,

wast - ed by our con - sum - ing path,

weep - ing the tears of poi - soned rain?

211 Where are the voices for the earth?

Where are the voices for the earth?
Where are the eyes to see her pain,
wasted by our consuming path,
weeping the tears of poisoned rain?

Sacred the soil that hugs the seed,
sacred the silent fall of snow,
sacred the world that God decreed,
water and sun and river flow.

Where shall we run who break this code,
where shall tomorrow's children be,
left with the ruined gifts of God,
death for the creatures, land, and sea?

We are the voices of the earth,
we who will care enough to cry,
cherish her beauty, clear her breath,
live that our planet may not die.

Shirley Erena Murray b. 1931

KINGSFOLD C.M.D.

Melody collected by Lucy Broadwood, 1858-1929
Adapted and Arr. Ralph Vaughan Williams, 1872-1958

1.Where my free spi-rit on-ward leads, well__ there shall be__ my way;

by__ my own light il - lu - mined I've__ jour-neyed night and day:

my__ age, a time - worn cloak I wear as__ once I__ wore my youth;

I__ cel-e - brate life's mys -ter- y; I__ cel- e - brate death's truth.

212 Where my free spirit onward leads

Where my free spirit onward leads,
well, there shall be my way;
by my own light illumined
I've journeyed night and day;
my age a time-worn cloak I wear
as once I wore my youth;
I celebrate life's mystery;
I celebrate death's truth.

My family is not confined
to mother, mate and child;
but it includes all creatures
be they tame or be they wild;
my family upon this earth
includes all living things
on land, or in the ocean deep,
or borne aloft on wings.

The ever spinning universe,
well, there shall be my home;
I sing and spin within it
as through this life I roam;
eternity is hard to ken
and harder still is this:
a human life when truly seen
is briefer than a kiss.

Alicia S. Carpenter b. 1930

ST PETER C.M.

Alexander Robert Reinagle, 1799-1877

1.Where sci - ence serves and art in - spires a strug - gling hu - man - kind, there truth and beau - ty point to God's hor - i - zons of the mind.

213 Where science serves and art inspires

Where science serves and art inspires
a struggling humankind,
there truth and beauty point to God's
horizons of the mind.

Where joys are shared and fears which once
lay hid in lives apart,
there love unlocks the doors on God's
horizons of the heart.

Where mind and heart together trust
the One who makes life whole,
there faith reveals in splendour God's
horizons of the soul.

O God, bring far horizons near,
complete the search begun,
so what we see and dream and what
we do, by grace, are one.

Jane Manton Marshall b. 1924

DIVINE MYSTERIES 66.66.88.66.

F. Stanfield, 1835-1914

1.Where shall I find that pow'r which makes the pla-nets move, and can I, in this hour, dis - cov - er per-fect love? Though I am in per-plex-i-ty, may I dis-cern in-fin-i-ty, and, though the glass be dark, of light see just one spark.

214 Where shall I find that power?

1st verse is with the music

Where shall I find that peace
which intellect exceeds,
and can I, in this place,
find what my spirit needs?
Though filled with fears I cannot quell,
may I escape my private hell,
and, though I cannot move,
be rescued by a dove?

Where shall I find that home
which calls me every day,
and can I, 'twixt the womb
and death, find out the way?
And though I, frantic, look around,
'midst clamour and despairing sound,
beneath that awful noise
I hear a still small voice.

What says this voice, now clear,
which I have long ignored?
Can I begin to hear
the wordless speech of God?
Vain chatter will I lay aside,
no longer filled with boundless pride:
the voice of God shall be
power, peace and home to me.

Peter Galbraith b. 1928

215 Where there is faith there is love

SZÉKELY ÁLDÁS (Székely Blessing)

Elizabeth H. Norton, b.1959

Words: Traditional Transylvanian

<u>Translation:</u> The English words are a translation of the original Hungarian

<u>Performance:</u> First time: Part 1 only; second time: Part 2 only;
                third time: both parts together.

<u>Hungarian Pronunciation:</u>   i = ee, é = ay, e = eh, sz = s, s = sh
                           cs = ch, o = oh, st = sht.

SCHMÜCKE DICH 88.88.D. Trochaic

Melody by Johann Crüger, 1598-1662

216 Wide green world

Wide green world, we know and love you:
clear blue skies that arch above you,
moon-tugged oceans rising, falling,
summer rain and cuckoo calling.
Some wild ancient ferment bore us,
us and all that went before us:
life in desert, forest, mountain,
life in stream and springing fountain.

We know how to mould and tame you,
we have power to mar and maim you.
Show us by your silent growing
that which we should all be knowing:
we are of you, not your master,
we who plan supreme disaster.
If with careless greed we use you
inch by extinct inch we lose you.

May our births and deaths remind us
others still will come behind us.
That they also may enjoy you
we with wisdom will employ you.
That our care may always bless you
teach us we do not possess you.
We are part and parcel of you.
Wide green world, we share and love you.

June D. Bell b. 1918

HEBDEN

David Dawson, b.1939

1.Winds be still. Storm clouds pass and___ si - lence come. Peace grace this time with har___ mo - ny.

Fly, bird of hope, and shine,___ light of love, and in calm let all find___ tran - quil___ i - ty.

217 Winds be still

Winds be still.
Storm clouds pass and silence come.
Peace grace this time with harmony.
Fly, bird of hope, and shine, light of love,
and in calm let all find tranquillity.

Birds fly high.
Lift our gaze toward distant view.
Help us to sense life's mystery.
Fly high and far, and lead us each to see
how we move through the winds of eternity.

Light shine in.
Luminate our inward view.
Help us to see with clarity.
Shine bright and true so we may join our songs
in new sounds that become full symphony.

Richard Kimball b. 1939

MACH'S MIT MIR, GOTT 88.88.88.

Melody: J. H. Schein, 1586-1630
Harmony: J. S. Bach, 1685-1750

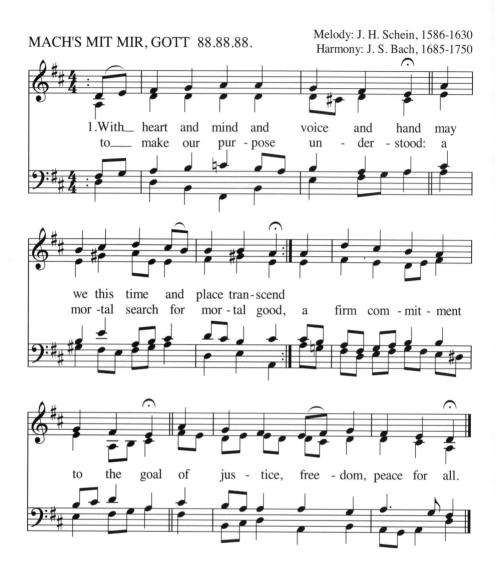

1.With heart and mind and voice and hand may
 to make our pur - pose un - der - stood: a

we this time and place tran-scend
mor -tal search for mor -tal good, a firm com -mit -ment

to the goal of jus - tice, free -dom, peace for all.

218 With heart and mind

With heart and mind and voice and hand
may we this time and place transcend
to make our purpose understood:
a mortal search for mortal good,
a firm commitment to the goal
of justice, freedom, peace for all.

A mind that's free to seek the truth;
a mind that's free in age and youth
to choose a path no threat impedes,
wherever light of conscience leads.
Our martyrs died so we could be
a church where every mind is free.

A heart that's kind, a heart whose search
makes love the spirit of our church,
where we can grow, and each one's gift
is sanctified, and spirits lift,
where every door is open wide
for all who choose to step inside.

Alicia S. Carpenter b. 1930

WHARFEDALE 11.9.11.6.

David Dawson, b.1939

1.You are the song of my heart in the morn - ing; you are the
dawn of truth in my soul; you are the dew of the
ro - se's a-dorn - ing; you are the wo - ven whole.

219 You are the song of my heart

You are the song of my heart in the morning;
      you are the dawn of truth in my soul;
you are the dew of the rose's adorning;
      you are the woven whole.

Yours is the grace to be steadfast in danger;
      yours is the peace that none can destroy;
yours is the face of the need-riven stranger;
      yours are the wings of joy.

You are the deep to the deep in me calling;
      you are a lamp where my feet shall tread;
your way is steep, past the peril of falling;
      you are my daily bread.

Yours be the praise of my spirit uplifted;
      you are the sea to each flowing stream;
yours are the days that are gathered and sifted;
      you are the deathless dream.

Kendyl Gibbons b. 1955

PACEM CORDIUM 86.87.5.

Jean Hytch

1.Your life is good, is good__ my friends, up - on your hearths a fire. Out - side the pleas of those who freeze, can your hearts not hear, not hear? Can your hearts not hear?

Music © Jean Hytch. Used by permission.

220 Your life is good

Your life is good, is good my friends,
upon your hearths a fire.
Outside the pleas of those who freeze,
can your hearts not hear, not hear?
Can your hearts not hear?

Secure and safe within your house
you hear the homeless plead.
They cry in vain and ask again
"Can your hearts not heed, not heed?
Can your hearts not heed?"

Your friends and family about,
in company you dwell.
The lonely ache, no comfort take,
can your hearts not tell, not tell?
Can your hearts not tell?

You have your solace, warmth and cheer,
but what of those out there
who hungry wait beside your gate?
Can your hearts not care, not care?
Can your hearts not care?

Kath Mayor

Words © Kath Mayor. Used by permission.

221 Alleluia, Amen

Anonymous

① Al - le - lu - ia, Al - le - lu - ia,

② A - - men. A - - men.

222 Building bridges

Contemporary English Quaker round

① Build - ing bridg - es__ be - tween our di - vi - sions, I

② reach out to you, will you reach out to me? With

③ all of our voi - ces__ and all of our vi - sions,

④ friends, we could make such sweet har - mo - ny.

223 Come, whoever you are

PILGRIMAGE

Lynn Adair Ungar, b.1963

① Come, come, who - ev - er you are, wan - der - er,

② wor - ship -per, lov - er of leav - ing. Ours is no car - a - van

③④ of__ des - pair. Come, yet a - gain come._____

Words adapted from Rumi (1207-1273)
Music © Lynn Adair Ungar. Used by permission.

224 Evening Breeze

Traditional

Eve-ning breeze, spi-rit song, sings to me when the day is done.

Mo-ther earth a-wa-kens me with the heart-beat of the_ sea.

225 Flaming chalice

Thomas Benjamin, b.1940

Flam-ing chal-ice burn-ing_bright, now you_ share with

us your light. May we al-ways learn to_ share_

with all_ peo-ple ev-'ry-where.

Music © Thomas Benjamin. Used by permission

226 From you I receive

Joseph and Nathan Segal

From you I re-ceive,_ to you I give,_ to-

ge-ther_ we share, and from this we live.

Words and Music © Nathan Segal, 1969. www.nathan.net. Used by permission.

227 Gathered here

GATHERING CHANT

Philip A Porter, b.1953

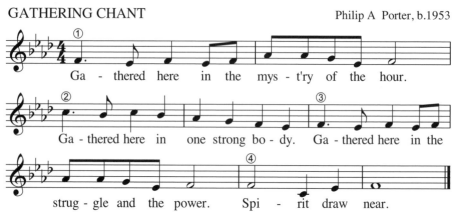

Ga - thered here in the mys - t'ry of the hour.
Ga - thered here in one strong bo - dy. Ga - thered here in the
strug - gle and the power. Spi - rit draw near.

Words and Music © Philip A Porter

228 Morning has come

Traditional

Morn - ing has come. Night is a - way.
Rise with the sun_____ and_ wel - come the day.

229 Rise up, O flame

CHALICE

Christoph Praetorius

Rise up, O flame_____ by_ thy_ light glow - ing,
show to us beau - ty,_ vi - sion, and joy.

230 Sing and rejoice

Traditional

Sing and re - joice. Sing and re - joice.

Let all things liv - ing__ now__ sing and re - joice.

231 When will the fighting cease?

GIVE PEACE

Melchior Franck, c.1579-1639

When will the fight - ing cease?

When will the fight - ing

When will we live in peace? When our

cease? When will we live in

Last time only

love breaks bound - 'ries. When will the

Last time only

peace? When our love breaks bound - 'ries. When

Note: The 3rd voice sings exactly the same as the 1st voice, starting in the middle of the 2nd bar. The 4th voice sings the same as the 2nd voice starting at the beginning of bar 3.

WORDS FOR WORSHIP

Hymns are by far the most frequent form of active congregational participation in worship. But other parts of the worship service can be a focus for group involvement. To that end we provide here a few *Chalice Lightings*, *Affirmations*, and *Benedictions*.

CHALICE LIGHTINGS

232   Kindling the flame holds kindly all memory.
Kindling the flame holds kindly all love.
Kindling the flame holds kindly all life.
Kindling the flame holds kindly all here.

Kay Millard

233   We open ourselves to worship today.
May the peace of this house bring us calm.
May the joy of this hour make our hearts glad.
May the challenge of this hour awaken our courage.
May the communion of this hour confirm our togetherness.

Dawn Buckle

234   This is our meeting house for worship, here we are a community connected by ties of faith and fellowship.
May the diversity of our beliefs be a blessing to share;
that all may grow in harmony with the Divine.

Celia Cartwright

235   We light this chalice to remind us of the shared cup of fellowship and the light of wisdom. The warmth of its glow reminds us of God's everlasting love.

Vernon Marshall

236 Friends, draw close.
Listen together. Sing together. Pray together.
Share the mysteries which never die, and the
silences that never cease. And as we share
and celebrate and worship, one in all, and all in each,
may we feel and know that we are being understood better
than we know and understand ourselves.

May we give to the winds our fears.
May we give to the world our faith.
May we give to Life our thanks and our service,
for evermore.

Benjamin Downing

237 We light this chalice to honour Jan Hus, burned at the stake
in 1415. He taught us:
"Love one another and always speak the Truth."
We light this chalice to honour Michael Servetus, burned at
the stake as a Unitarian in 1553.
We light this chalice to honour Francis David who died in
prison in 1579. He taught us:
"You need not think alike to love alike."
We light this chalice to honour all who passed the torch of
our free faith.

Richard Boeke

238 As is our custom here, we light the chalice – and see!
The flame of truth burns bright,
fed by the vision of each of us,
rising from the heart of us all.
Let its light shine out as our lives shine out,
brightening the dark places of the world,
bringing wholeness and peace.

Joy Croft

AFFIRMATIONS

239 We would make this place a temple of the heart's desire;
built from the hewn rocks of our individuality
and from the sure mortar of our shared understandings,
an unwalled, unbounded temple
wherein all people may praise, in tones of joy,
the Highest Things that give life meaning and worth,
and draw us ever onward beyond our known selves.

We would make of this place a centre of meeting for the lost and
uncertain, that we may gain renewed hope to face life's
joys and sorrows with enterprise and forbearance,
that we may know also a deep gratitude for all the
opportunities of growing.
We would make of this place a home in which dwell
Love, Peace and Honour:
In this deep covenant let us join, now, and for evermore.

Frank Clabburn

240 Look to this day-
for it is life, the very life of life.
In its brief course lie all the verities
and realities of your existence:
the bliss of growth,
the glory of action, the splendour of beauty.
For yesterday is but a dream,
and tomorrow is only a vision,
but today well lived makes every yesterday a dream of happiness
and every tomorrow a vision of hope.
Look well, therefore, to this day.

From the Sanskrit

241 Lead me from death to life,
from falsehood to truth.
Lead me from despair to hope,
from fear to trust.
Lead me from hate to love,
from war to peace.
Let peace fill our hearts,
our world, our universe.
Peace, Peace, Peace.

The Peace Prayer

242 May the deeds we do with our hands,
and the words we speak with our lips,
and the thoughts that we think with our minds,
and the things we feel in our hearts,
be at all times worthy of the divine spark within us.

Traditional

243 This is my church. It is composed of people like me.
We make it what it is.
I want it to be a church that is a lamp to the path of pilgrims,
leading them to Goodness, Truth and Beauty.
It will be if I am.
It will make generous gifts to many causes,
if I am a generous giver.
It will bring other people into its worship and fellowship,
if I bring them.
It will be friendly if I am. Its pews will be filled, if I fill them.
It will do great work if I work.
It will be a church of loyalty and love, of fearlessness and
faith; a church with a noble spirit – if I, who make it what it
is, am filled with these.
Therefore, I shall dedicate myself to the task of being all of
these things I want my church to be.

From 'Songs for Living'

244   This place is a house of the spirits,
the spirits of our forebears in the Unitarian faith,
who proclaimed the eternal values of
Freedom, Reason and Tolerance,
and on every convivial occasion proposed a toast
to Civil and Religious Liberty the World Over.

May we be happy to boast of our spiritual freedom,
and to work for the spiritual freedom of all those
whose faith in life is confined and mocked,
showing by our actions what we believe in our hearts.

Peter Sampson

BENEDICTIONS

245   Friends,
Thank you.
I say thank you from us all to us all.

Thank you for being here.
Thank you for your singing,
and your silence,
your presence and your prayers.

For it is by your being,
that we all can know the depth of Being.
It is by your singing and silence,
that we can know a unity in togetherness.

And it is by your Presence,
that we can know that other Presence,
here.
Being together.

Thank you.

John Midgley

246 May the calm be widespread.
May the sea glisten like the greenstone.
And may the shimmer of sunlight
ever cross your pathway in life,
now and always.

Maori Valediction

247 In the name of us all
let there be Peace and Love among us.
May the skies be clear.
May the streets be safe.
In the name of us all
let there be peace.

Keith Gilley

248 Dimming the flame lets memory rest.
Dimming the flame lets love grow again.
Dimming the flame sets life free to live.
Dimming the flame lets all go in peace.

Kay Millard

249 As we leave this sanctuary
may the holy music linger in our ears.
May the poetry of the spoken words stay in our minds.
May our spirits remain uplifted.
May our lives be blest.

Dawn Buckle

250 Let us go in peace-
to live together in harmony,
to see beauty in everything,
to know wonder in each passing moment,
and to walk gently with our God. Amen

Celia Cartwright

Index of Subjects

Index of Subjects

Index of Subjects

Index of Subjects

Index of Subjects

Index of Subjects

Index of Subjects

Index of Subjects

Index of Subjects

Index of Subjects

Index of Subjects

Alphabetical Index of Tunes

Alphabetical Index of Tunes

Alphabetical Index of Tunes

Alphabetical Index of Tunes

Metrical Index of Tunes

Metrical Index of Tunes

Metrical Index of Tunes

Metrical Index of Tunes

Metrical Index of Tunes

Index of Composers, Arrangers and Music Sources

Index of Composers, Arrangers and Music Sources

Index of Composers, Arrangers and Music Sources

Index of Authors

Index of Authors

Index of Authors

Haughen, Marty b.1950
49 God of day and God of darkness

Hewett, Phillip
176 To sunlit ranges of life's peaks

Hildegard of Bingen 1098-1179
67 I am that great and fiery force

Hill, Andrew McKean b.1942
4 All that is abundant living
17 Caring God, your watching o'er us
22 Come strong God and walk beside us
25 Conscience, guide our footsteps
26 Dancing sweet heart
59 Ground, it's time for your rebirth
84 Justice for persons and for different nations
92 Let us renew our covenant
94 Let us welcome Channukah
101 May I use my hands with care
129 Ours is a gift received from source
133 Play trumpet, cello, harp and flute
134 Praise God for Michael
146 Speaking truth in love, we gather...
150 Stillness, creeping through this place
159 The green grass brings the air to life
160 The highest goodness is like water
184 We are here in stillness
186 We are travellers on a journey
196 We sing the faith

Hopson, Hal b.1933
174 Though I may speak with bravest fire

Hungarian Unitarian
81 Isten, God of our confessing

Idle, Christopher M. b.1938
166 The works of the Lord
60 Here I am, all alone

Isaiah 55 adapted
40 For you shall go out in joy

Jones, Richard G. b.1926
20 Come all who look to God today

Kaszoni, Jozsef trs.
81 Isten, God of our confessing

Kimball, Richard S. b.1939
217 Winds be still, storm clouds pass

Knight, Sydney Henry 1923-2004
121 O yearning hearts

MacKay, Karen b.1952
73 If every woman in the world

Marshall, Jane Manton b.1924
213 Where science serves and art inspires

Mason, Roger
142 Shining through the universe

Masten, Ric 1929-2008
88 Let it be a dance we do

Mayor, Kath
220 Your life is good, is good my friend

McCready, Tom
71 If all the prophets were silent

McDade, Carolyn b.1935
24 Come, sing a song with me
148 Spirit of life, come unto me

Michaels, Christine Doreian b.1942
173 Though gathered here to celebrate

Michell, Myrna
77 In the morning, when the dawn leans
171 This is the moment

Mikelson, Thomas Jarl S, b.1936
181 Wake now my senses

Mitchell, Lyanne
147 Spirit of earth, root, stone and tree

Morn, Mary Katherine & Shelton, Jason
42 From the light of days remembered

Index of Authors

Index of Authors

Index of First Lines of Hymns

Index of First Lines of Hymns

Index of First Lines of Hymns